THE FOUR HORSEMEN OF THE APOCALYPSE

THE GREATEST WARNING OF THE NEXT 10 YEARS

STEVE CIOCCOLANTI

PRAISE FROM LEADERS

"I love this book The Four Horsemen. I believe every Christian everywhere should read it. It is obvious that Steve Cioccolanti has done a tremendous study. Get ready to be blessed challenged and taught!"

DR. MARK T. BARCLAY
Author & Founding Pastor
Living Word International Church

"The Four Horsemen is a stand-out work that bridges faith, history, and current events. Steve Cioccolanti's ability to decode complex prophetic symbols makes this a must-read for anyone seeking to understand the times. One thing that stuck with me was the danger of spiritual deception disguised as righteousness, like the white horse in Revelation. This book is both a wake-up call and a guidepost—rich in prophecy, grounded in truth and written with conviction."

Dr. WAYNE CORDEIRO
Pastor & Author
New Hope International

"Steve has managed to provide amazing detail and timing on each of the four horsemen with deep inside on ways to prepare for these upcoming end-time events. This is a type of book that is hard to put down as you can't wait to go to the next chapter, as it also reveals how ready you are (or not), and what to do to not just survive but thrive in these soon upcoming and end-time world shaking events depending on your understanding and revelation."

DR. DAVID HERZOG
Mass Evangelist & Author of "Glory And The End Times"

"I love that Steve Cioccolanti recognizes the importance of seeing scripture through a Hebraic lens and he understands the importance of knowing the Times and Seasons. He also acknowledges the biblical calendar with all the appointed times. Steve Cioccolanti's new book The Four Horsemen of the Apocalypse is not only a great read but an eye-opener as well! If you want a deeper understanding of where we are in history biblically, this book is a must read! Thank you Steve for a phenomenal book!"

PASTOR MARK BLITZ
El Shaddai Ministries
Author of "Blood Moons" & "The Final Tyrant"

*To my wife who said,
"You must finish this book.
This will change the world."*

THE FOUR HORSEMEN OF THE APOCALYPSE:

The Greatest Warning of the Next 10 Years

Published by Discover Media www.discover.org.au

Copyright © 2025 by Steve Cioccolanti. All rights reserved.

No part of this book may be reproduced in any form, except for the use of brief quotations in a book review. Unless otherwise noted, all Scripture quotations are taken from the (ESV) English Standard Version. Copyright © 2001 by Crossway Bibles. Used with permission.

Scriptures taken from other versions are marked as below and used by permission:

(NASB) New American Standard Bible®. Copyright © 1960-1995, 2020 by The Lockman Foundation. Used with permission.

(GNT) Good News Translation® (Today's English Version, Second Edition). Copyright © 1992 American Bible Society.

(KJV) King James Version. Public domain.

(NET) New English Translation or NET Bible®. Copyright ©1996-2017 by Biblical Studies Press.

(NKJV) New King James Version of the Bible. Copyright © 1979, 1980, 1982. Used by permission of Thomas Nelson, Inc., Publishers.

(NLT) New Living Translation. Copyright © 1996, 2004, 2015 by Tyndale House Foundation. Used by permission of Tyndale House Publishers, Inc.

Cover design by *Selena Sok*.

Hardcover ISBN 978-1-922273-61-1 (B&W inside, available worldwide)

Paperback ISBN 978-1-922273-59-8 (full color, USA & UK only)

E-book ISBN 978-1-922273-60-4 (full color, worldwide)

Printed in the U.S.A.

CONTENTS

Preface: The Importance of Change	1
1. Would History Turn Out Differently?	7
2. True & False Prophets	22
3. Can We Predict the Future?	41
4. The Bible in One Minute	56
5. Introducing the Book of Revelation	59
6. When Do the 7 Seals Open?	64
7. The Flags	78
8. The White Horse	89
9. Sorcery in the Last Days	99
10. A New Timeline	107
11. The Red Horse	114
12. The Eclipses & the Sign of Jonah	131
13. The Black Horse	148
14. Goshen	165
15. The Green Horse	178
16. Seals 5, 6, 7	201
17. The Time of Jacob's Trouble	208
18. Shmittah Cycles	214
19. Top End Time Advice	219
Bestsellers by Steve Cioccolanti	231
Acknowledgments	233
Meet Steve Cioccolanti	235

PREFACE: THE IMPORTANCE OF CHANGE

THE IMPORTANCE OF THIS MESSAGE

IF THE CONCLUSIONS of this book are correct, six things should be understood from the outset:

1) The Bible was right, not me.

2) Several other interpretations of the end times will be falsified, or at least need to be adjusted. This is a heavy burden that kept me from sharing the book until now. I do not intend to embarrass anyone. I respect the prophets, pastors and teachers who've gone before me. I really do. We needed their sacrifice and wisdom. They taught us the best they could know at the time they taught it. But given the closeness of the Lord's coming, we can now see some things more clearly than they did.

3) You should not make life-changing financial decisions based on the roadmap of this book. I will make my own decisions based on the information I've been shown, but what's good for me may not be good for you. Please seek wisdom, pray about what our Heavenly Father wants you to do, and don't blame anyone including yours truly for what you decide. I can be many things to

you—a prophet, a pastor, a teacher—but I'm not your financial advisor.

4) You should not panic, but you should make quality decisions about the way you're living your life. You should deem life on this earth as more precious, more finite than it seems, and realize that you may be more accountable than you thought.

5) Be careful about getting what you wish for. Many of us prayed for Charlie Kirk to grow Turning Point and influence the halls of academia and the highest echelons of leadership. He did, and they murdered him for it. Many of us prayed for Donald Trump to return to power. He did in 2025. But what's to come during his four years will be an opportunity for the enemy to saddle a lot of heat and a lot of blame on the President, MAGA, and the "Christian nationalists." From the mid-point of his presidency onwards, things will go as no one expected, unless they read this book.

Christians need to do a lot more than win one election. Christians need to know God's timeline and live like they heed a Parent's warning. **Our Heavenly Father is telling us what He wants and when He wants it.** The things He wants to accomplish in America are in my book, **"Trump's Unfinished Business: 10 Prophecies to Save America."** The timing in which they can happen are in this book.

In life, **timing is everything.** Those who resist God's timing, who baulk at or oppose the transition, will risk being left behind in God's Plan.

6) If you're a leader, you will be judged by a higher standard. **James 3:1** warns, *"My brethren, let not many of you become teachers, knowing that we shall receive a stricter judgment."* You should be more honest, seek God more deeply, seek the welfare of others more than your own, and be careful that you do not abuse your power. One of the worst evils that's about to be exposed and punished is the secret abuse of power. I guarantee it.

You will see many prominent Christian pastors' downfall. They taught the Bible, but they lived double lives. This will occur not because they could not repent or could not be redeemed (they certainly can), but because God's promise is coming to pass: *"For the time has come for judgment to begin at the house of God; and if it begins with us first, what will be the end of those who do not obey the gospel of God?"* (1 Peter 4:17)

A TOUGH PILL TO SWALLOW

This message will be a kind of religious "red pill" (a cultural reference from the movie "The Matrix"). It may be hard for religious people who have built their lives, churches or ministries on an interpretation that they learned from their Bible school, a bestseller book, or someone else. While I am not trying to embarrass those who thought they taught the Bible, I am suggesting that some of our cherished assumptions may not be as Bible-based as we thought. They may be extrapolations from the Bible at best, or our personal wishes at worst.

I am very aware of the pain that these adjustments can cause and I don't intend to bring on pain. I mean very much for change to be positive, to be a pleasure. This is how I try to live my life: if I need to change, whether I choose it or God brings it my way—I welcome it. I see God's refining work, shaping me into a better person, as a pleasure. The Lord is gracious because He refuses to let us stay the same.

WHY A PARADIGM SHIFT IS NEEDED

The Lord has demanded paradigm shifts periodically. His Word remains exactly the same before and after. However, our perspective of His Word broadened dramatically after each shift. Let me give you 3 instances from the past, present and future.

From Old Testament to New Testament

The transition from the Old Testament to the New Testament was perfectly Biblical, yet we lost the majority of Bible teachers during the transition, notably 99% of all the Jewish rabbis!

Why?

What God demanded of Old Testament believers during the time of transition was a broadened perspective about the qualifications of salvation. The Jewish leaders were too narrow in their understanding of redemption.

Prior to the transition, the Jews believed correctly that they were God's chosen people. During the transition, God wanted the Jews to take up their role as a "light to the Gentiles" and "to bring salvation to the ends of the earth" (Isaiah 42:6, 49:6, 60:3, Acts 13:47). It seems so obvious now, after the transition from Old to New Testament, that this was God's Plan all along.

Why would the Creator God save only one nation and ignore 192 other nations? Why would the Savior (the Messiah in Hebrew) come from Heaven to save only one ethnic group and not all ethnic groups? After the transition, believers who accepted that God is for every nation, the Bible is for every nation, the Messiah is for every nation, became known as "Christians."

These are no longer radical ideas, and those people who refused to follow God's transition now seem outdated at best and "Pharisaical" at worst. Yet there remains a minority of Bible teachers who still believe (incorrectly) that Gentiles cannot be saved apart from converting to Judaism, and that the Messiah belongs only to the ethnic Jews instead of to all the Gentiles who repent of their sins and believe in the blood sacrifice of Christ.

The point is this: the transition was difficult, but God absolutely demanded it, and those who went through it came out better people.

PREFACE: THE IMPORTANCE OF CHANGE

From Centralization to Decentralization

The Lord demanded another transition from the centralization of Roman Catholicism to the decentralization of the Protestant Reformation. If you're Catholic, please don't be turned off by a bit of history.

There was a time when the Catholic Church excommunicated and persecuted Bible translators. It sounds unfavorable to your denomination, but it's true. The Catholic Church led the charge in pursuing, torturing and executing anyone who dared to translate the Bible from Latin into the "vernacular" or common language of the people. It's ironic as the Bible was not even written in Latin to begin with. It was recorded in Hebrew, Aramaic and Greek, so what the Roman Catholics were guarding was a translation of the original into Latin (called the Vulgate). They should have been the most open to translating the Bible into other languages.

Christians who wanted to read and understand the Bible for themselves eventually won and they were called "Protestants" because they *protested* against many dogmas of the Catholic hierarchy. Today, not a single Catholic Pope, Bishop or mass attender would murder a Protestant for reading the Bible. God has enlarged our perspectives. Hidden truths then seem obvious now.

It seems self-evident now that God wants the Bible in every language, that God is fluent in every language, and that God can speak to everyone in their own language. The transition during the 1500s was difficult, but God absolutely demanded it, and those who went through it came out better people.

Those who still believe that the Bible must be read in Latin only, or Hebrew only, or King James English only, are the minority, and have no influence over the larger Body of Christ. God loves them. God is not trying to marginalize them, but they marginalize themselves, because God wanted to broaden the perspective of the majority of believers.

From the Status Quo to the New Millennium

There's coming a transition from the New Testament to the Millennial Kingdom of Christ described in Revelation chapter 20. Only those who have repented of their sins and trusted in the Savior will make it in. Furthermore, those who have obeyed Christ in this life will be put into power with eternal ranks of authority. It is a subject worth an entire book on its own. I promise to write it. But while I have much to say about the next 1000 years, the subject of this book is only the next 10 years.

If we can convince the majority of Christians to make a small transition through the next 10 years, I am sure the Lord will be very pleased to show us the next 1000 years.

CHAPTER 1
WOULD HISTORY TURN OUT DIFFERENTLY?

THE BOOK you're holding will not cover old territory—we have no time for that.

Eleven years before the COVID pandemic, I **predicted in 2009** that the 2020 pandemic would come and described the specifics of the anti-Christ agenda—control, martial law and mask mandates. It's on **YouTube**.

| Predicted in 2009

Before the lockdowns, the Lord told me to prepare an online church. I tried to tell a few of my peers who were pastors. None of them believed me.

At that time, YouTube was new (it went online in 2005), Twitter was new (2006), and most pastors were familiar with only Facebook (started at Harvard in 2004). The very concept of **"social media outreach"** was met with resistance, being equated with "sheep stealing." In other words,

| Discover's Channel

pastors saw social media not as a genuine space for ministry, but as a distraction and a waste of time.

I recall this vividly because I was convinced the Lord had told me to minister to people on social media, yet none of my peers agreed. Was I wrong?

At that time, I was unaware that the 2020 pandemic and online church would become connected. But in hindsight, it now looks obvious. So obvious that once the pandemic started, pastors were asking me how I was getting a million views on my YouTube videos and how they could do it too. For most, it was too late for them to catch up to me. The Lord had given me a head start.

This is the purpose of prophecy. This is also the pain of carrying the prophetic burden—of seeing and preparing for things ahead of time, before other people understand. By definition, *prophecy challenges the status quo*. It's not what people are used to. Sincere, learned, wonderful, and moral people will oppose prophecy. They often won't understand it till it's too late.

They don't realize the prophet is like **headlights** on the church's car. They prefer to turn them off. During the day time, they can get away with it. But as soon as it rains or the world becomes dim or dark, they'll be grasping again to turn on the highbeams and fog lights.

My advice became so self-evident that every church I knew scrambled to bring their church services online (though I still do not consider one-way video streaming to be "online church," but that was the best most churches could do). My long-term premonition seems so obvious in hindsight that most thriving churches now offer an employed position called **"social media pastor"** or some equivalent. If anyone had predicted that in 2004, a mere 20 years ago, they would have been laughed to scorn. Who would have budgeted church funds for such a role? It's not a "real" ministerial position…until it became very real and necessary.

This book will tell you what's going to happen in the next 10 years. When the new events unfold, every pastor, prophet and those who lived through the COVID lockdowns will say it was obvious. Some will be asking themselves, why did they not learn from the first warning. If you read this book cover to cover, you will be ahead of the curve.

This book also will tell you what's NOT going to happen during the next 10 years. What do I mean? Based on the timeline God has shown me, I should be able to eliminate some rumors, deceptions, options and distractions out of my mind because of my assurance of what's *not* going to happen. Here are some examples of how useful it would have been if Christians had known something was *not* going to happen:

- **The housing bubble of 2008 was *not* going to be the end of American prosperity and dominance.** National home prices fell 30% from their peak in 2006 to the bottom in 2012. The average American panicked. I know one Australian man flew to Florida to pick up a piece of land in Florida at Leigh High Acres. This man wasn't rich. The market began to recover and boomed during COVID. National home prices rose 40% from January 2020 till August 2022. Less than 10 years later, he made a five-fold return on investment, and without having to rent or deal with tenants.
- **Trump was *not* going to win the 2020 election.** Put another way, VP Mike Pence was *not* going to question the electoral votes of disputed states, he was *not* going to "return" those votes to the states for review, and he was *not* going to delay ratification on January 6, 2020. Had Trump known, he would have chosen a better VP. In the years following, there have been at least 200 convictions of voter fraud, absentee ballot fraud and misconduct in public office. It would have been helpful to know the Supreme Court was *not* going to scrutinize the results of the 2020 election, was *not* going to allow examination of

fraud allegations, and was *not* going to order a statewide audit of votes in any swing state. There was precedent for the Court to intervene in *Bush v. Gore (2000)*. The Florida Supreme Court had ordered a statewide manual recount to determine voter intent in cases of unclear ballots (the "hanging chads"). The U.S. Supreme Court issued a stay on the recount, then overturned this lower court's decision due to lack of uniform standards to evaluate voter intent, thus securing Bush's certified win. In *Texas v. Pennsylvania (Dec 2020)*, the state of Texas sued 4 other states—Pennsylvania, Georgia, Michigan and Wisconsin—over alleged unconstitutional election changes (e.g. expanding mail-in voting and relaxing mail-in rules without legislative approval). Under Article III, the Supreme Court has exclusive jurisdiction over suits between states, and could have issued an emergency stay to halt certification and hear arguments. Instead, the justices dismissed the challenge, thereby not questioning and not altering the certified results in favor of Joe Biden. Had Trump known the Supreme Court would not even entertain his plea for justice, he would have nominated 3 different justices—as advised in my book ***Trump's Unfinished Business: 10 Prophecies to Save America.***

- The Lord showed me that the justices did not represent the U.S. population or God's will, and He showed me who to nominate to fix it. Even though the book made it to the White House, President Trump did not receive it or did not follow the prophetic word.

Trump's Unfinished Business

Congress also did not challenge the results of the 2020 election, but that was not under Trump's control. What was under his control were his choices for Vice President and Supreme Court justice nominees. How history could have turned out differently if Trump had known what would *not* happen.

It is helpful to know what is *not* going to happen. For this reason, you will find that I was in great peace about certain events and times. In my teachings (some posted on YouTube with timestamps for you to verify) I made several predictions about what's *not* going to occur.

- **Ukraine was *not* going to win the war against Russia.** My prediction was against the narrative pushed out by all mainstream media and repeated by Christian leaders. They claimed that with Western backing, Ukraine would advance to a swift victory. Background: U.S. and European powers had provoked Russia for decades by breaking their promises and treaties, and expanding NATO membership closer to Russia. Russia responded by invading Ukraine on 24 February 2022. Christians started changing their social media profiles and avatars to blue and yellow to show solidarity with Ukraine, creating a new breed of social justice warriors, rallying to an unrighteous cause in the most corrupt country in Europe. Hatred for Russia ramped up, exacerbated by the "Trump-Russia collusion hoax," a narrative the media disseminated *ad nauseum*, then quietly retracted.[1] Prophecy watchers eyed Russia as an apocalyptic expansionist power.
- I assured my listeners God loves both sides and it's vain

---

1. CNN retracted the story linking Anthony Scaramucci (a Trump ally) to a $10 billion Russian investment fund: https://www.washingtonpost.com/lifestyle/style/the-story-behind-a-retracted-cnn-report-on-the-trump-campaign-and-russia/2017/08/17/af03cd60-82d6-11e7-ab27-1a21a8e006ab_story.html

to get involved on the wrong side. Ukraine is the most corrupt country in Europe, so Christian leaders were rooting for the wrong team. I don't hate Ukrainians; I don't want them to die in a war they can't win. I told believers I had zero trust in the former comedian/actor Volodymyr Zelenskyy who shut down churches, merged all major TV channels into one state-controlled "United News" to supposedly combat Russian "misinformation," jailed political opponents and postponed elections indefinitely. These are not the hallmarks of "democracy."

- As early as April 2, 2022, I posted **"Ukraine & the VIRGIN MARY | Is PUTIN Winning or Losing?"** In it I predicted, "The war in Ukraine will last longer than most expect, will produce supply chain disruptions, and will amplify the inflation that's already present. In the end, Putin will prevail in Ukraine. The biggest losers in Ukraine will be the Ukrainian people and Western investors and consumers."

Ukraine...Is PUTIN Winning or Losing?

- Contrast this with **Pat Robertson** (Founder of Christian Broadcasting Network or CBN) who claimed on March 3, 2022 that God told him the war in Ukraine fulfills Ezekiel 38 and Putin was leading a Russian coalition to invade Israel, "He's being compelled by God. He went

---

Washington Post amended headlines, added notes, and removed large portions of two articles published in March 2017 and February 2019. Both relied on the anti-Trump Steele dossier. This fell short of a sincere apology for influencing the 2020 election with unverified claims from the opposing party (Democrats). Fox reported on WP's quiet reversal on November 12, 2021: https://www.foxnews.com/media/washington-post-corrects-removes-reporting-steele-dossier

WOULD HISTORY TURN OUT DIFFERENTLY?

into the Ukraine, but that wasn't his goal. His goal was to move against Israel, ultimately. It's all there [referring to Ezekiel 38]. And God is getting ready to do something amazing and that will be fulfilled."[2]

- This is an American-centric theory that has been proven wrong again and again, yet American preachers keep repeating it. I greatly respect the work of CBN, especially the spread of *Super Book* the children's animation in different languages. With due respect, Robertson should have retracted it, but alas he passed away on June 8, 2023, at the age of 93, before he could make it right. I always give the benefit of the faith to ministers who are alive. I do not comment about them by name because even if they're wrong—as long as they're alive—they can make it right. But once they're dead, we honor their memory by reviewing their lives for lessons learned.

- The U.S. prophecy community is littered with unscriptural prophecies which are American cultural-assumptions-turned-to-Gospel. With these religious conjectures, mockers put the Church to shame for its lack of discernment and for jumping on spiritual bandwagons that go nowhere. I do not follow the American hype. Perhaps it is to your advantage, my reader, that you get from me an "outsider's perspective." I grew up with four major religions in the same household. I have lived in, traveled to, and/or led tours through almost 60 counties. I don't have a denominational bias. I don't have an American bias. I have a Bible bias. I'm pro-Jesus and pro-human.

- On September 22, 2022, I posted "**The RED HORSE of**

---

2. https://religionnews.com/2022/03/14/russia-ukraine-war-some-pastors-wonder-about-end-of-days/

the Apocalypse | 5 LIES About Ukraine & Russia that bring us on the brink of WW3." I shared 5 lies pushed by the mainstream media and the mainstream church. "Number one: that Russia is losing the war because it didn't capture Kiev in the first week. This is an American military doctrine, which is to use overwhelming force on countries incapable of defending themselves. This American doctrine has failed and has not won a war in our lifetime. It just doesn't work anymore. It's failed in Afghanistan [where we couldn't win against goat herders], it's failed in Iraq, and it will fail with Russia. You cannot just use sudden overwhelming force from the sky and think you will win a war." Why was this prophetic intel more important than even military intel? Because if world leaders knew the prophetic word that Ukraine would *not* win, and Russia would *not* invade Israel, then these nations could have saved the following amounts they pledged to Ukraine:

The RED HORSE...5 LIES About Ukraine

- USA $125 Billion;
- E.U. €52 Billion euros;
- Canadian C$12.2 Billion;
- Japan US$13 Billion;
- Australia A$1.48 Billion.
- If the People had believed in Bible-inspired, Spirit-filled prophecy, instead of getting led astray by empty hype, we could have not lost 400,000 lives on both sides, not wasted $205 Billion globally on Ukraine, and spent the money on local infrastructure and emergencies like the Maui Fires of August 2023, Hurricane Helene Floods of September 2024, and Los

WOULD HISTORY TURN OUT DIFFERENTLY?

Angeles Fires of January 2025. Many of those victims are still waiting for help while Zelenskyy gets billions.

- **Trump was *not* going to end the war between Russia and Ukraine during his first day in office or first year or first two years.** Neither Zelensky nor Putin intended to do what Trump wanted. What could explain this? Come with me and I will show you why in the chapter on the Red Horse.
- **Ezekiel 38 was *not* going to happen in 2024, 2025 or 2026.** Background: Iran had been conducting a proxy war against Israel through funding and training terrorist organizations, namely Hamas (Gaza Strip), Hezbollah (Lebanon), and Houthis (Yemen). Meanwhile the regime deceived the International Atomic Energy Agency (IAEA) by concealing nuclear material and activities at several sites. Fearing the development of a nuclear weapons program, Israel made a preemptive strike on Iran's military and nuclear sites on June 13, 2025.
- Iran retaliated by sending 525 ballistic missiles and 300 drones into Israel. On June 22, 2025, President Trump authorized the use of bunker busting bombs to destroy Iran's nuclear facilities. Operation Midnight Hammer was an unprecedented success: about 125 planes flew 18 hours to Iran unchallenged by their air defense, dropped 14 Massive Ordinance Penetrators (MOPs) and 24 cruise missiles with surgical precision on *Fordow, Natanz,* and *Isfahan*, completing the mission in about half an hour, then flew 18 hours home without a single casualty or loss of aircraft. Iran quickly agreed to terms of peace. The Twelve Day War ended on June 24. As the Lord showed me, there was no Ezekiel 38 War.
- In prophecy circles and prophecy conferences, any conflict with Iran immediately sparks anticipation for

the fulfillment of Ezekiel 38. To me, it's as silly as expecting a Depression every time the stock market corrects. We should be more mature than that. We should be looking for more corroboration with other Scriptures and God's timeline. But Christians paid to listen to teachers who stoked their excitement about the soon fulfillment of Ezekiel 38. They bought books about Revelation and Ezekiel which rehashed old misleading claims. I was not moved by the sensationalism. I am moved by God's timeline. I could see that these speakers were not aware they were in the wrong timeline because they didn't understand the book of Revelation, especially the 4 horsemen. It's as important to know what will *not* happen as what will happen.

- **Russia is *not* going to invade Israel.** I have said this repeatedly despite prophecy teachers jumping up and down every time there is war in the Middle East. Countless popular figures have claimed, "Russia is Gog," "Russia is going to invade Israel," "This is going to be the Ezekiel 38 War finally." Some Christians are gullible enough to follow this teaching that has no basis in Scripture, history or geography. "*Rosh*" is not Russia because it sounds like Russia in English. *Rosh* in Ezekiel 38 is the Hebrew word for "head," like *Rosh Hashanah* is "head of the year" or new year. I gave "9 Reasons Russia is NOT Gog-Magog of Ezekiel 38-39" back on 7 November 2014.

- **I accurately ruled out a "rapture of the Church" on September 23, 2025.** Several prophecy watchers were convinced something significant would happen on this date. I was not. They said the Feast of Trumpets would coincide with the UN meeting on the 23rd (to be precise, the 80th General Assembly met from 19th-28th). They said the UN would recognize the 2-State Solution and

Palestine as a sovereign nation. I said they would not. How did I know? The prophetic timeline God gave me showed a completely different timing. We were years away from the possibility of Rapture or Tribulation. I do not predict when the Rapture will occur, but I can predict when the Rapture *cannot* occur. It cannot occur for at least the next 9 years. When I warned Christians of this false hope, I received the this text from a pastor:

> "I think you better repent for having a negative mindset about our loving Father. Jesus, our Bridegroom is really coming back this month. With a heavy burden, I am delivering this message. For not testing every prophecy, you have grieved the Holy Spirit."

- o He did not apologize afterwards. A friend would have congratulated me, in humility, for pleasing the Holy Spirit and guiding the Church away from speculative date-setting.
- **The USD is not going to collapse in 2023, 2024, or 2025.** I stood toe-to-toe with economic advisors, financial prognosticators, and gold sellers who predicted the collapse of the US dollar too early and I said, "*No. It won't happen yet. It's not the right time.*" Some said it would happen at the end of 2023, then the end of 2024. I said to one, "*May be you're right. But what happens if you're wrong? Will you admit you got the timing off?*" He said to me, "*I can't be wrong.*" Well, that's the definition of deception. Any of us can be wrong. Many times I wish I was wrong. I wish I was wrong about the attack on America before September 11, 2025, which ended up being fulfilled by the murder of Charlie Kirk on September 10, 2025. Who would want to be right about

something like that? But *so far*, up to now, the predictions the Lord allowed me to release have come to pass. I predicted there would *not* be a USD collapse or Depression in 2023, 2024, 2025, or 2026. How many respectable voices contradicted my prophecy!

- **Robert Kiyosaki**, author of "Rich Dad Poor Dad" the #1 bestselling financial book of all time, predicted in 2022 that the U.S. real estate bubble would burst imminently, leading to a broader economic meltdown and USD devaluation. U.S. housing prices rose 10% in 2022. The dollar did not collapse.
- **Gerald Celente**, Founder of Trends Research Institute, said in December 2018 that "the long bull market is over," predicting an immediate stock crash and USD devaluation. The S&P rose 29% in 2019. From December 2018 to October 2025, the S&P has given a 168% price return on investment, not counting any dividends paid during those years. The USD has been strengthened against all currencies, as I predicted throughout 2023-2025.
- **Tucker Carlson**, formerly host of the #1 cable news program, has been on the record predicting the collapse of the USD since 2023, the year I said the USD would strengthen. Tucker cautioned that U.S. foreign policy, especially sanctions on Russia, was accelerating de-dollarization and emboldening BRICS nations to reject the USD in trade. While I agree with Tucker we should stop treating Russia as an enemy, I did not agree that the USD would collapse. The reverse occurred.

- **Trump Tariffs would *not* cause a global stock market crash in 2025.** I was convinced of this due to God's Timeline which is to be revealed in this book. I watched mainstream media in Japan, Singapore, and

Australia lambast Trump as a dangerous leader who didn't understand economics. If anyone believed the news commentators around the world, they would think that their investments were about to crash and hyperinflation was about to hit. Instead, the stock market rose and prices declined. Despite being wrong, the global news' *response* to Trump had the desired effect: it scared voters in other countries.

- On May 5, 2025, I sent a message on Telegram, "*Both Australia and Canada have been lost in the past few days to radical left wing ideologues. Yet young men have been swinging to conservatism and traditionalism. What happened in those federal elections?*
- *The Trump tariffs scared internationals off because they don't understand them historically or strategically. Scared people vote for left-wingers. Strong independent people vote for less government intrusion.*
- *This is one reason @realDonaldTrump needs an international Christian advisor. Trump has now lost 2 major ally countries to leaders who oppose him and hate him with their guts.*
- *…Now Trump has to deal with 2 English speaking countries whose leaders erode freedom, love censorship, ban fossil fuel, push dubious green tech and want digital ID, digital control, and digital surveillance as fast as possible. Where are the Christian advisors to the President?*"

• A pastoral word or prophetic message to the international churches that a crash was *not* coming could have had a positive effect on calming the electorate and encouraging them not to vote out of fear. Trump's tariffs worked. China pledged $500 Billion in U.S. investments and reduced barriers on American agriculture; Mexico pledged $300 Billion investment in U.S. border facilities and migration control tied to trade; Vietnam, Indonesia, the Philippines and South Korea all agreed to trade deals by April-May 2025. Trump was elected to put America first; other nations should elect similarly capable leaders, not corrupt ones who sell their nation's farmland and future to foreigners, invite unskilled labor in, impose control and restrict free speech.

The prophetic model the Lord has shown me has a reliable track record of predicting what will happen and what will *not* happen. Few prominent pastors or prophecy teachers currently believe this paradigm shift. I am unaware of anyone among them who teaches what I'm about to share with you. They may likely be the ones to oppose me the most. I've been through this before.

Recall I suggested they should start online church long before COVID hit. I got a tepid response but continued with online church until COVID vindicated us as a ministry. I must continue to write what God tells me and sound the alarm to wake up the sleeping church. We don't have much time.

> May Salazar: Thank you Pastor Steve for this message; you bring PEACE to my HEART about soo many things going on..I'm always waiting and watching for your messages like a hawk LOL…your always so calm and peaceful on how you explain things like prophecy..God bless you Today and always May the Lord Protect you and your family…I hope one day soon I will have the opportunity to meet you all

> Pastor Steve: For sure, come on one of our Christian tours… before the Door closes: www.discover.org.au/tour

THE PEOPLE'S TIMELINE

Just as the People validated my social media outreach and online church, ordinary readers like you will help corroborate the veracity of the Lord's 10-year map. It will expose false prophets, dispel lies, alleviate fears, and leave you in a better position to experience peace and minister to others. This spiritual paradigm shift will come from the "grassroots" and not from the "gatekeepers" of religion. The religious leaders will adopt what you adopt. They will speak what you speak. They won't want to miss out.

CHAPTER 2
TRUE & FALSE PROPHETS

THE PREDICTIONS in this book will not be vague—meaning, without measurable, time-based specifics. They will be Bible-based and come in 3 phases. They will be falsifiable. That means if any phase is wrong, you'll know it year by year, for the next 10 years (2025-2035).

EPIC FLOPS

The fact is, I recognize that timing is a difficult subject—ask any trader who's tried to "time the market" by picking tops and bottoms. It's virtually impossible, though some have gotten close.

It's good enough to know the trend and follow a few rules to make a successful trade. "Buy low, sell high" will make you wealthy. "Buy the bottom, sell the top" will make you go broke and lose sleep at night. It's too perfectionist and unrealistic a goal. It's not necessary to succeed.

Just as a good financial mentor will teach you to recognize patterns and trends, so too this book will give you a lot of tools to successfully understand prophecy, without date-setting the Second Coming.

We're not going to "time the Top." We will be out of the market before then![1]

No one who's predicted the Second Coming of Christ has been right so far. Edgar Whisenant's book "*88 Reasons Why The Rapture Will Be in 1988*" is probably the most notorious example of a recently failed prediction, followed by the cringeworthy "*89 Reasons Why the Rapture will be in 1989.*"

Even the mainstream, popular end-time teacher Hal Lindsay was confident Christ would return no later than 1988. Harold Camping, president of Family Radio, stuck with the 1988 date and claimed it was the "end of the church age." He predicted the rapture would occur on May 21, 2011, followed by the Second Coming on October 21, 2011. Ronald Weinland, leader of the Church of God, believed he was one of the two witnesses of Revelation 11. (He wasn't.) He predicted the Second Coming would occur on September 29, 2011. When it failed, he revised it to May 27, 2012.

Recently, South African pastor Joshua Mhlakela predicted the Rapture and Second Coming would happen on September 23-24, 2025 (*Rosh Hashanah* 5786 on the Hebrew calendar). Having studied and taught the subject extensively for 25 years, I publicly ruled out the possibility of a rapture in 2025. It did not fit the Biblical timeline I'm about to show you. Several online followers accused me of not expecting Christ's coming any more. That's not true! Even though I was proven correct, and the date passed without any significant event, Mhlakela revised it to October 7-8, 2025. Christians would forgive him if he had repented.

Another notorious example from history was William Miller's prediction that Christ would return to earth in 1843. When it failed, he revised it to 1844. The "Great Disappointment" ensued, when most followers abandoned the eschatology of Millerism. Rather

---

1. In this parable, the "Top" is the Second Coming, and exiting the market near, but before, the top is the "Rapture." One's theory of the Rapture timing has no impact on the Biblical timeline in this book. We are focusing on events that are soon to come, before the Tribulation.

than admit wrong, William Miller justified his prediction by claiming that it was in fact fulfilled by the cleansing of the "Sanctuary in Heaven," an event which could not be seen and could not be verified by anyone (other than Miller).

His protégé Ellen White embraced Miller's explanation and co-founded the "Seventh Day Adventists," a splinter group of Millerites dedicated to end-time teachings that vary from the common views of orthodox Christian groups, such as the astounding claim that the anti-Christ "mark of the beast" is worshipping Jesus on Sunday.

OVERVIEW OF PREDICTIONS

Acutely aware of how these miscalculations make a mockery of prophecy, I am not predicting the Second Coming of Jesus Christ in 10 years. I am not suggesting the Rapture will occur in 10 years. I am not claiming that the world will end in 10 years.

What I am saying, through the evidence that will be presented in this book, is that none of those things can happen within the next 10 years.[2] This may disappoint some, but it empowers others. Ten years will go by quickly, yet this period gives us enough time to adjust our lives and obey God. It gives us enough time to put Jesus first.

---

[2]. Those who hold the doctrine of "imminence" say that (a) "Jesus can come back any time" and (b) "nothing needs to be fulfilled before Jesus comes back." If we apply those standards to the First Coming of Christ, we can see that it's patently false. In response to (a) Jesus could not come any time; He had to present Himself as the Sacrifice for sin exactly on the Day of Passover and resurrect exactly on the Holiday of Firstfruits. In response to (b) several things needed to precede His Coming, notably the 69 weeks of years (483 years) had to transpire as per Daniel 9:25. The same will be true of the Second Coming. Once you understand God's Feasts, God's calendar, God's timeline, and God's prophecies, you can no longer believe Jesus' Second Coming is "imminent." At the very least, "this Gospel of the Kingdom" must "be preached in all the world as a witness to all nations, and then the end will come." (Matthew 24:14) Christ cannot come yet because the Gospel has not yet been preached to all ethnic groups.

I am also claiming that we have been blessed by the Lord—we have a 10-year roadmap straight from the Word of God. We know what's going to happen in the next 10 years (and counting down for those who pick up this book later).

Beyond that, I have some premonition and educated guesses, but we'll keep those for my avid followers inside our **online church**. It's a growing community of Bible lovers, prophecy watchers, and practical preppers.

This book is meant firstly to be an introduction to God's Timeline for prophecy watchers; secondly, for the believers to share Christ with seekers; and thirdly, for everyone to prepare their lives to believe Jesus and obey the Lord before He returns.

MODERN PROPHECY

The Apostle John wrote in Revelation 19:10, "...For the testimony of Jesus is the spirit of prophecy." If testifying about who Jesus is in my life is still for today, then prophecy is still for today. Paul said, "Pursue love, and earnestly desire the spiritual gifts, especially that you may prophesy." (1 Corinthians 14:1) Peter agreed this is God's will in his first sermon to the Church:

> **Acts 2:17-18**
>
> "And in the last days it shall be, God declares, that I will pour out my Spirit on all flesh, and your sons and your daughters shall PROPHESY, and your young men shall see visions, and your old men shall dream dreams; **18** even on my male servants and female servants in those days I will pour out my Spirit, and they shall PROPHESY.

To prophesy simply means to speak by the unction or

inspiration of the Holy Spirit. It must always line up with the Word of God; since the Holy Spirit wrote God's Word (2 Timothy 3:16, 2 Peter 1:21), He won't contradict Himself. Any prophecy that contradicts God's Word is from a demonic source.

On the surface, there's nothing controversial about prophecy: God speaks. Why wouldn't He? God speaks to us primarily through His written Word, called the Holy Bible, but many things He truly spoke and did are *not* recorded in the Bible. The Apostle John made sure we knew this:

> **John 20:30**
> Now Jesus did many other signs in the presence of the disciples, which are not written in this book;

> **John 21:25**
> Now there are also many other things that Jesus did. Were every one of them to be written, I suppose that the world itself could not contain the books that would be written.

Not everything God said and did was recorded in the Bible. Only what is essential and necessary for our salvation and eternal wellbeing was recorded. Jesus underscores this point when He said:

> **John 16:12**
> I still have many things to say to you, but you cannot bear them now.

Does that mean we cannot hear from Jesus any more? No! Jesus then proceeded to tell us about the Holy Spirit and His ministry.

> **John 16:13-15**
> When the Spirit of truth comes, he will guide you into all the truth, for he will not speak on his own

authority, but whatever he hears he will speak, and he will declare to you the things that are to come. **14** He will glorify me, for he will take what is mine and declare it to you. **15** All that the Father has is mine; therefore I said that he will take what is mine and declare it to you.

The consensus of Scriptures shows that God wants to speak to Christians today. We get to know Him first by His written Word, but the more we believe His Word, the better we will hear His Holy Spirit. What the Spirit of Christ speaks through us is called prophecy.

Prophecy often centers on justice, which is usually accompanied by a warning and a verdict, hence it tends to come across as futuristic. The prophet Micah said what true prophets feel:

> **Micah 3:8** (NET)
> But I am full of the courage that the Lord's Spirit gives and have a strong commitment to JUSTICE. This enables me to confront Jacob with its rebellion and Israel with its sin.

Micah could care less how futuristic his sermons were. He cared for justice. All true prophets do. John the Baptist was called the greatest of Old Testament prophets, yet there's no record of him predicting the distant future. There are several statements of John preaching justice.

> **Luke 3:7, 17**
> ..."You brood of vipers! Who warned you to flee from the wrath to come? [Then introducing the Messiah who was not yet revealed, John said] **17** His winnowing fork is in his hand, to clear his threshing floor and to gather the wheat into his

barn, but the chaff he will burn with unquenchable fire."

John said in effect, "Someone is coming to bring justice. He will separate people—the repentant from the stubborn. He will judge people, so repent while He still gives you a chance." When John said this, it seems within *days* Jesus came and got baptized by John.

The Gospel of John makes it very clear that when John the Baptist was asked by the Jewish priests and Levites if He was the Messiah, he denied it and pointed to somebody else. Then "the next day" he saw Jesus coming toward him and said, "Behold, the Lamb of God, who takes away the sin of the world. This is he..."! (John 1:29-30) So John's prophecy had one of the shortest gaps between utterance and fulfillment.

John announced someone coming, and the next day, there He was! This is the spirit of the forerunner. This is the speed of Elijah. In the last days, we speak, and it happens. We write, and it's fulfilled. We predict, and it's already done. The gap between prophecy and judgment becomes shorter and shorter. I will show modern examples of this in the next chapter.

20TH CENTURY PROPHET

Demos Shakarian, founder of Full Gospel Businessmen, recounts the story of the Armenian Pentecostal revival in the early 20th century in his book *The Happiest People on Earth* (1975). In the village of Kara Kala near the Caspian Sea, the Lord sent a boy of Russian origin to warn them of a day when "every Christian in Kara Kala would face terrible danger."

At the age of 11, Efim Gerasemovitch Klubniken received a vision during a 7-day prayer vigil (a time of fasting and waiting on the Lord). Efim saw a vision of charts and a message "in beautiful handwriting." Even though he was illiterate, he transcribed it onto paper, producing a manuscript in Russian characters (verified by literate villagers as beyond the child's capability). The prophecy warned of:

- An impending "**unspeakable tragedy**" for the entire region, where every Christian in Kara Kala would face terrible danger.
- All residents must flee to a land across a great sea (his hand-drawn map accurately depicted the Atlantic Ocean and pointed to the United States).
- Refugees should land on the east coast of America but not settle there; instead, continue to the west coast, where God would bless them, prosper them, and make their descendants "a blessing to the nations."

Efim had never seen a geography book or map. The first time he shared this prophecy (around 1867), he was not taken seriously.

27 years later, a confirming event foreshadowed his prediction: the **Hamidian massacres** of 1894-1896. An estimated 80,000-300,000 Armenians were systematically slaughtered by Kurds and Turks over 3 years. The term Hamidians refer to the forces and supporters of Ottoman Sultan Abdul Hamid II who implemented a pan-Islamic policy. Hamid used irregular Kurdish cavalry units, Ottoman soldiers, police, and local Muslim mobs to suppress Armenian nationalist movements.

News of the 1896 **Constantinople massacre** would have traveled to Kara Kala. In 3 days, Muslims killed 6,000 Armenian Christians. But the villagers still didn't believe the prophecy. After all, the capital city was far away from their little place. They felt safe where they were.

47 years later, when Efim was 58 and still known in the village as the "Boy Prophet," he said, "It's time. We must flee to America. All who remain here will perish." A handful of families from the Pentecostal revival left for the U.S. in 1914. Most people stayed.

Those who fled reached America safely and later heard reports of the **Armenian Genocide** (1915-1923).

In Kara Kala, every inhabitant (the entire Christian population) was killed during the 1915 massacres. Nationally, over 1.5 million Armenians (out of 2 million in the Ottoman Empire) died in the village massacres and "death marches" into the Mesopotamian desert (from starvation, exposure, and executions).

Armenia is considered the first Christian nation on earth. King Tiridates III officially adopted Christianity as the state religion in 301AD, predating the Roman Empire's legalization of Christianity under Constantine by the Edict of Milan (313). Yet Armenia fell under Ottoman control for 543 years. When it looked like her people could be free, she was absorbed into the Soviet Union for 70 years. Armenia did not regain independence until the dissolution of the Soviet Union in 1991.

While there are some "failed" or fake prophecies, there are many more genuine ones. A supernatural warning repeated over 47 years saved a small number of believers from the Armenian Genocide. The Christians who listened to the Boy Prophet truly thrived on the west coast of America. Demos' father bought over 200 acres of land and built the world's largest private dairy with 3,000 cows milked daily during the 1940s-50s.

The Armenian believers continued to blend faith and enterprise, which laid the blueprint for "Full Gospel Businessmen." The supernatural sustained them and was an essential part of their daily life. The Demos family relied upon the prayers and advice of the charismatic prophet Dr. Kelso Glover. During a tuberculosis (TB) outbreak in a 40-acre facility, Dr. Glover's intercession healed over 1,000 cows with no recurrences for 20+ years.

9 LESSONS FOR US

1. Modern prophets exist.
2. They are treated much like ancient prophets—the people liked to hear predictions about a good future, but they hated to hear about justice and judgment. Rejection of prophecy was so common in the Church, Paul had to instruct believers, "Despise not prophesyings." (1 Thessalonians 5:20 KJV)
3. Many Christians hold the belief that if an area has many Christians, they cannot be harmed.
4. Many Christians believe that if there are enough Christians around, only blessings will flow and they will never need to be inconvenienced by an Exodus. They assume God would never ask them to move to a foreign country.
5. Biblical Prophets routinely told believers to move out of a good area in anticipation of great danger.
    - Moses and Aaron told the Jews to leave Egypt, where many were apparently happy and comfortable (Numbers 11:5 *"We remember the fish we ate in Egypt that cost nothing, the cucumbers, the melons, the leeks, the onions, and the garlic."*).
    - Jeremiah told believers to go to Babylon and submit themselves to the Babylonians for 70 years. (Jeremiah 29:7 *And seek the peace of the city where I have caused you to be carried away captive, and pray to the Lord for it; for in its peace you will have peace.* The Hebrew concept of "peace" or "shalom" refers to welfare and prosperity.) Get along with the foreigners. Be a light to them and share the Torah. Do business with them and seek mutual prosperity (29:4-10, 25:8-12).

- Jesus told both Jews and Christians to flee Jerusalem in 32AD. Roman General Gallus surrounded Jerusalem in 66AD, but after 2-3 weeks he suddenly retreated. Most Christians believed Jesus' prophecy, left Jerusalem and saved their families. Most Jews did not believe and stayed. The Christians looked foolish for 4 years. When Roman General Titus came to lay siege again on Jerusalem, around Passover of 70AD, the unthinkable happened—300,000 Jews were slaughtered and 97,000 enslaved. Despite having the Holy City and the Holy Temple, Israel ceased to be a nation.

6. Warnings do not have to make sense when you first hear them. You should judge the source. If the person is trustworthy, don't doubt. Many prophecies don't make sense and even seem foolish until such time as the fulfillment.

7. God is gracious to give multiple warnings. In both Jerusalem and Armenia (eastern Anatolia at the time), believers were given a prelude to destruction.
    - Jerusalem was surrounded twice in 66AD and 70AD. The second invasion was worse.
    - The Ottoman Empire had massacres in 1894-96 and in 1915-1923. The second one is always worse.
    - If you wonder how Christians could ignore a boy prophet's warning that was partially fulfilled 27 years after the delivery, then again 47 years later, recall it's been only 24 years since God's end time warning to America on September 11, 2001. Did many Christians or pastors change since that date? Churches were initially filled for a couple of weekends, but then people forgot Bible prophecy and went "back to normal." Inertia and status quo are powerful forces. If

the Attack in 2001 was a similar warning to us as the Hamidian massacre was to the Armenians, then the real attack on the U.S. has not even come. It would be due in 2028 and 2048. How many pastors today would have the spiritual sensitivity to connect, for their flock's sake, the 2001 attack to a worse attack in 2028?

- In 2025, America had its first public execution of a Christian: **Charlie Kirk**. A temporary revival ensued; American youth going back to church. I celebrate this, yet I also know it'll be short-lived. *The second attack is always worse.* Many prophets have warned of the unthinkable—beheadings of Christians in America.
- Pastor **Dana Coverstone** of Kentucky had 3 dreams in 2020. In the third, he saw Christians arrested and executed in public squares by foreign invaders. He saw guillotines and crowds chanting against the "infidels."
- **Henry Gruber** of International Harvest Ministries reported a vision in the 1990s that he saw foreign invasions leading to Christian persecution and mass beheadings in detention camps for people who refused the "mark of the beast (the Anti-Christ)." He saw "guillotines in FEMA camps" and Christians singing as they were executed.
- **Sadhu Sundar Selvaraj**, a prophet from India, was given a vision in 2016 in which he saw American Christians beheaded in stadiums by Islamic radicals during a civil war-like scene, with the government complicit. He described angels recording the martyrs' names for heavenly rewards.
- Read the Chapter "The Black Horse" for a strategy of what Christians can do.

8. The length of time between prophetic warnings and their fulfillment appears to be contracting. In the Old Testament, prophets warned of events that took from a thousand years down to 70 years to be fulfilled. Jesus' prophecy about Jerusalem's destruction took 38 years to come to pass. Efim's prophecy took 27 years to see its first and partial fulfillment. I have seen many predictions in this ministry fulfilled within days and hours. Our video **"WAR is IMMINENT"** was posted on October 6 and fulfilled on October 7, 2023.[3]

9. Be prompt to obey prophecy and warnings. Delays can cost more than you're willing to pay. Jews who waited till the Holocaust to get out of Germany no longer had an escape. As Chris Martenson, co-founder of Peak Prosperity, says, **"Better a year early than a day too late."**

War is Imminent

THE PROPHET: THE MOST MISUNDERSTOOD MINISTRY

The true prophet's ministry has been greatly misunderstood. The Bible does not show us examples of prophets who speak at conferences and say, *"God is about to do something in this nation."* Prophets are personal advisors to leaders.

- Samuel advised Saul.
- Nathan advised David.

---

3. I posted a warning about the October 7th Hamas Attack and of the Gog Magog War 8 years before October 7, titled "15 Year Old Secular Jewish Boy Nathan's Vision of WWIII on Blood Moon: Gog Magog Future of Israel."

- Elijah advised Ahab and Ahaziah.
- Jonah advised the King of Nineveh (Assyria)
- Daniel advised four kings: Nebuchadnezzar II, Belshazzar, Darius the Mede and Cyrus the Great. (Daniel was one of the greatest because he advised a great number of leaders.)
- Dr. Kelso Glover advised the Shakarian family and their dairy business.
- Charlie Kirk could be called a prophet to President Donald Trump.
- I advise pastors, school principals, and various business leaders. My book "Trump's Unfinished Business" is direct advice for world leaders.

Being a prophet is not a feeling, a style of speaking, or fortune-telling. It's a job—a calling from God. Prophets give specific, actionable advice or warnings to leaders, whether they are pastors, school principals, business owners, politicians, or kings.

Prophets do this because they see things from a higher perspective than the leaders, who need to focus on solving problems, casting vision, raising funds, recruiting talent, meeting targets, identifying waste, going to court, pleasing partners or stakeholders, and disciplining or firing troublemakers. A prophet spends time with God and sees and knows things leaders cannot see. For instance, Saul missed the mark, but he couldn't tell and his subordinates couldn't help. Only Samuel could tell Saul. Trump missed the mark in his first term, then he suffered lawfare (legal persecution) for 4 years. He could have avoided most of those pains by following the prophetic template already written in "Trump's Unfinished Business." Any world leader could do the same. Those 10 policies will always remain God's agenda for a Golden Age.

The Bible tells us that Jesus gave 5 ministry gifts to us. God knows we need them.

> **Ephesians 4:8, 11**
> **8** Therefore He says: "When He ascended on high, He led captivity captive, And gave gifts to men."
> **11** And He Himself gave some *to be* apostles, some prophets, some evangelists, and some pastors and teachers,

Here's the easiest way for people to understand the 5-fold ministry offices. We all speak the same message—the Gospel and the Word of God, but we are sent to speak to different audiences.

- Prophets speak to leaders.
- Evangelists speak to sinners and seekers.
- Pastors speak to church members.
- Teachers speak to Christians.
- Apostles speak to whoever God sends them to.

It may be helpful to translate these old concepts into modern parlance:

- Prophets act as advisors and consultants to leaders—religious, business or political. They preach the Gospel and teach the Word day-to-day like any other ministry gift.
- Evangelists are recruiters and marketers of the Kingdom.
- Pastors are your coaches and personal therapists.
- Teachers are the trainers in any organization. They write curricula and disseminate information in your churches, schools, businesses. They must themselves be trained to handle the Word of God honestly.
- Apostles are the pioneers and entrepreneurs in the Body of Christ. They start things and go to new places. Often they are itinerant missionaries traveling to establish churches, schools, or even a whole new community.

- It was taught in my Bible school that missionaries are the modern apostles. After 30 years traveling to 60 countries, I no longer believe this to be entirely true. It used to be true in the 1700s and 1800s.
- Not all missionaries today qualify as apostles. Many missionaries now go to places that already have an established church presence and they spend 3-5 years learning a foreign language and culture. They often get frustrated and run out of funds quickly. They are actually evangelists or teachers who should simply work under a local pastor. They are not pioneers, do not produce, do not innovate, and would be crushed under the pressure of pioneering.
- I believe some Christians are uncelebrated apostles. They make 100 calls a day, organize conferences for 1000s to attend, network with top leaders fearlessly, and eat pressure for breakfast.
- They are good with names, are generous with contacts, and network for a living. (Think about how many people Paul names in his letters and how many people he connected and raised up.) Christians who are highly productive like Paul operate in the apostolic.

We need true prophets today who truly understand the end times. The true ones will be misunderstood and falsely accused. They see concrete things ahead of time. Leaders know they need this heavenly intel.

The false prophets do not merely make wild predictions. That would be easy to spot. The false prophets tend to appeal merely to your emotions and hype up their talk, "God's about to do something great! The best is yet to come!" Imagine advising the President, "God's about to do something." Well, what is it? "I don't know, but the best is yet to come." No.

For instance, the Lord has given me specifics for the leader of the free world. On March 21, 2024, the Lord gave me a prophetic message I posted: **"The Only 2-STATE SOLUTION God Will Bless‼ VISION of WAR & PEACE in Israel, Gaza & Middle East."**

Gaza has no chance of peace until it's turned into a Christian nation next to Israel—a place of refuge for the most persecuted Christians in the world, starting with the Arab Christians, and not forgetting the Indian, Pakistani, Nigerian and Sudanese Christians. Soon we can add to them Canadian, Australian, and British Christians, who have no First Amendment rights or protection of free speech.

Welcome them to Gaza. They will never attack Israel. Jews will have peaceful friends forever next door. The economy would boom. It would fulfill Bible prophecy, because Gaza belongs to the territory of Judah, which is Jesus' tribe. Where else would Christians, children of the Lion of the Tribe of Judah, live in the Promise Land?

No pastor has seen this solution because it's not their job. We read the same Bible, but we see different solutions for different people. Pastors should not fear the prophetic—the true gift of the prophet. If my prophecy is right, pastors will be needed in Gaza. We should rather be working together.

No politician has seen this solution because it's not from human reasoning; it's revelation. It's revealed by God. Prophecy cannot be contradicted. If you oppose this plan, you can be the richest man in the world and have the most powerful military on earth, and your plan will flop!

On the other hand, you can be a simple leader who obeys God, and though you may not have the richest economy or the most advanced weapons, your plan will succeed! Whenever you line up with God, Heaven's grace, favor and resources will be poured out on you. The rise and fall of people, families and empires cannot be understood only from a social, political, psychological or economic point of view. Sodom was a prospering city that attracted Lot, but through sin was suddenly wiped out by fire from the sky (meteorites).

Pompeii (near modern Naples, Italy) was a bustling port town with beachside villas, aqueducts, and a 20,000-seat amphitheater. It prospered for 159 years until Mount Vesuvius erupted on 24 August 79AD and buried its inhabitants under 6 meters (20 feet) of ash. The pyroclastic surge (sudden ash) came at 300-500mph. There was no time to run. It killed instantly.

Archaeologists have unearthed evidence of the vices for which judgment came on Pompeii: 35 brothels, erotic art at homes, phallic symbols outside of homes, over 200 dice used in games and gambling, graffiti with insults and explicit sexual content, and pagan charms and amulets. Did God warn them?

There was a major (5-6 Magnitude) earthquake in 62AD, a full 17 years before the devastating eruption. For four days leading up to the explosion, locals witnessed that wells dried up, springs altered in composition, and animals fled (birds and dogs). Hours before the eruption, a steam plume was seen 20 miles high.

Ignoring the warnings, one admiral of the Roman fleet, Pliny the Elder, decided to go investigate the eruption rather than flee. His last words were, "Fortune favors the brave." It was hubris. He died from toxic gases and a heart attack (per modern analysis). In a twist of irony, the eruption occurred on a festival day *Vucanalia*, a pagan holiday honoring *Vulcan* the god of fire. I call it "poetic justice," when the punishment is unmistakably fitting and divine. It wasn't Climate Change on the 24th of August—it was worshipping the devil. All Christians should have left town that day and not partaken in any celebration. Sometimes we don't understand why we should obey God, but we should still obey!

Some of the things you will read in this book could not be understood prior to 2020. COVID triggered the final redemptive countdown. Some things are sealed, as the prophet Daniel was told by the angel Gabriel, "Go your way, Daniel, for the words are shut up and **sealed** until the time of the end." (Daniel 12:9)

Daniel's metaphor is the exact same one John used in the Book of Revelation: the **first seal**, which releases the first Horseman of the Apocalypse. Combining Daniel and John's prophecies, we see a clear picture:

- Someone at the right time will break open the seal.
- We won't know what the first horseman is until the first seal is broken.
- The first seal won't be broken till the *"time of the end."*

This book will honor the spirit of prophecy and show you evidence the first seal has been broken, the horsemen are riding, and they're already impacting the economies, nations and the Church.

And yet, the Tribulation has *not* started. This may challenge some old, favorite timelines people have been taught, but it's time for a sound Biblical update.

> Spencer: Pastor Steve, As a former JW [Jehovah's Witness], I want to thank you for the hours of sermons you put online that I watched to help un-indoctrinate myself and come to learn what the Bible really says. I love that you speak truth clearly and with a loud voice, unwaveringly and fearlessly. I find that inspiring in my faith walk to also be courageous and bold. I was baptized in a good non denominational church in 2019 and I have made a promise to follow Jesus the rest of my life. I love Him and I'm grateful you let Him speak through you. Thank you!

CHAPTER 3
CAN WE PREDICT THE FUTURE?

IF THIS BOOK WERE KFC, you're about to get the secret recipe. You're going to be given the secret sauce—the method to decode prophecy for at least the next 10 years (2025-2035). The principles apply far beyond 2035. Once you are adept in handling the Word with wisdom, you should be able to discern beyond 2035 as you approach that time. You will know where to look...*how* to look. For the purpose of this book, we begin with the obvious.

The most well-known Biblical motif in all of prophetic literature —the "**4 Horsemen of the Apocalypse**"—will be indelibly etched in your mind so that you will be able to compare the 4 horses to current events as they are reported on the news. You will whisper to yourself, *"There it is!"* You will try to convince your loved ones, *"I told you so."* While some will be persuaded, others will not believe you.[1]

God intended for the "4 Horsemen of the Apocalypse" to be the most common word-picture or metaphor in the Bible. It's so

---

1. To see lost ones saved, follow the "6 Steps to Save Your Family" contained in Chapter 4 of the book "Get Prayers Answered."

common that non-church-goers know of it. It's used in everyday language, including the news. Examples:

- Canadian clinical psychologist **Jordan Peterson** refers to the 4 Horsemen as though they were "psychological warnings against societal collapse." He views restrictions on free speech as signs of social decay. He ardently opposes compelled speech in Canada's Bill C-16 and advocates for free speech.
- American Jewish professor at the University of Washington and relationship expert **John Gottman** appropriates the New Testament term to popularize a secular concept of the "Four Horsemen of Marital Failure." Gottman identified Criticism, Contempt, Defensiveness and Stonewalling as four behaviors that forecast divorce with over 90% accuracy.
- **Alex Jones**, the controversial and fearless investigative journalist, refers to the 4 Horsemen more literally. He takes them to mean "harbingers of globalist destruction." He refers to actual people like Barack Obama, Bill Gates, Klaus Schwab, George Soros and/or their successors as the quartet planning global control and depopulation.
- Libertarian author and gold investor **Doug Casey** is also literal in his interpretation. He aligns surprisingly well with the Bible when he wrote: "It's as if the world's governments decided to unleash the Four Horsemen of the Apocalypse (Pestilence, War, Famine, and Conquest)... The Four Horsemen are saddling up"[2] and "The four horsemen of the apocalypse are stalking humanity in earnest."[3] His timing for them is now. I

---

2. https://internationalman.com/articles/doug-casey-on-the-controlled-demolition-of-food-and-energy-supplies/
3. https://internationalman.com/articles/doug-casey-on-the-growing-threat-of-nuclear-war/

believe it helps not to be predisposed to a favorite position to discern the timeline correctly. (We'll cover this in the Chapter "When Do the 7 Seals Open?")

- Gizmodo published an article on December 23, 2024 that refers to SpaceX,[4] Palantir[5], OpenAI[6] and Anduril[7] as the "New Four Horsemen of the Apocalypse."[8]
- Back in 1983, evangelist **Billy Graham** ventured into eschatology by releasing a book titled *"Approaching Hoofbeats: The Four Horsemen of the Apocalypse,"* in which he warned of moral decay and the threat of nuclear war. It's hard to dispute that warning sinners of impending judgment is not an essential part of preaching the Gospel! When a mainstream Baptist preacher such as Billy Graham referred to the Four Horsemen to save sinners, the metaphor is undeniably captivating.

This book will explain God's Timeline, including the 4 Horsemen's meaning, like you have never heard it before. I have attended conferences where my teaching was quoted on stage or printed verbatim. I have seen the images I created for my Keynote slides 13 years ago published in another author's book without citation to my work. I've seen them used on various YouTube clips that did not reference the original source. One repurposed video got

---

4. SpaceX was founded in 2002 by Elon Musk.
5. Palantir was founded in 2003 by Peter Thiel, Alex Carp and others. One of their goals is to centralize our personal data for the government, an essential step to the Anti-Christ Beast system.
6. OpenAI was founded in December 2015 by Sam Altman, Elon Musk, and others. It was originally a non-profit for AI research. Musk stepped down in February 2018 to focus on his own AI now called Grok.
7. Anduril Industries is an American defense technology company founded in 2017 by Palmer Luckey, the creator of Oculus VR.
8. https://gizmodo.com/spacex-palantir-and-openai-reportedly-teaming-up-to-score-some-sweet-sweet-defense-contractor-cash-2000542646

more than 12 million views! Truly, I rejoice that I am plagiarized. English preacher Charles Caleb Colton wrote in 1820, *"Imitation is the sincerest form of flattery."* Whether by honesty or by crookedness, God's Word is getting to the people. The Apostle Paul experienced the same emulation and shared his feelings about it:

> **Philippians 1:15-18**
>
> Some indeed preach Christ from envy and rivalry, but others from good will. **16** The latter do it out of love, knowing that I am put here for the defense of the gospel. **17** The former proclaim Christ out of selfish ambition, not sincerely but thinking to afflict me in my imprisonment. **18** What then? Only that in every way, whether in pretense or in truth, Christ is proclaimed, and in that I rejoice.

Though many have taken to spread the message the Lord gave to me many years ago, long before I heard anyone else talk about it in this way, I can tell you that their message is incomplete—they only got a part of it right. The Lord showed me many more things about what's to come and how to prepare. After 25 years of teaching eschatology (end time prophecy) in Bible schools, churches, conferences and on **YouTube**, I can tell you this is no longer theory.

It's actionable intel from Heaven—Glory to the Messiah, His Word and His Holy Spirit!

Based on insights in this book, you will be able to make practical, profitable, and possibly life-saving decisions. How do I know?

| @DiscoverMinistries

I didn't know at first.

I proved it out over the course of 25 years before revealing it to the world. You can verify this ministry's track record. I do not share many predictions or prophecies publicly. I believe the main job of a prophet is to preach the Gospel, teach the Word, and minister to the sick. John the Baptist was called the "greatest of prophets"[9] and there's no record of him making a new prediction. He preached repentance and God's Kingdom, and pointed to the Messiah. I am careful about what I share, fearing the Lord. By the prophetic model revealed in the Holy Scripture, the Lord allowed me to:

- Predict **11 years in advance** (2009) the pandemic by which a virus would be released, mask mandates would be enforced, and martial law (lockdowns) would be declared.

  | 11 years in advance

- In 2009, we could not yet post a video "proof of prophecy" on YouTube, as YouTube was created in 2005 and our ministry joined it in 2010. I was not active on YouTube till 2012 when I heard the Lord say audibly to me, *"Get on YouTube!"* From early on we have been a video ministry. One of our core values is "redeeming technology for Christ." So we re-posted my prediction recorded in 2009, and the proof that it's genuine is I looked a lot thinner and younger. It may not satisfy everybody, but that's the truth.
- All I predicted was fulfilled to the detail, beginning in 2020, when the world was introduced to the globally-coordinated rollout of unvalidated health policies and COVID-19 vaccines. Almost the entire world was forced into lockdowns, social distancing, and mandatory vaccination. In the aftermath, studies show no discernible difference in the spread of COVID in states

---

9. Matthew 11:11 and Luke 7:28.

that enforced masks and vaccines, and states that did not.[10] The global harm should never be forgotten:

- Non-compliant people were persecuted socially and economically—some losing their livelihoods.
- Children lost years of structured learning, socializing, sports, play time, and many became myopic staring at screens. Boys especially craved routines.
- Nurses and soldiers were among those who lost their jobs without compensation. Churches closed down.
- Many died of vaccine-related injuries. For instance, a study based on U.K. data titled *Mortality risk after COVID-19 vaccination: A self-controlled case series study* (Peer-reviewed in Vaccine Journal, 2024), found an increased risk of cardiac-related deaths in young males (18–39) within 28 days of mRNA vaccination.[11] Such studies are few, and who will pay for them? The CDC is funded by pharmaceutical interests. When someone died suddenly after taking the COVID-19 vaccine, the cause of death was always listed as COVID, not vaccines. CDC reviews never show cause-effect patterns. *We will never be told an accurate number of such deaths.*
- While the poor and middle-class suffered, the COVID pandemic era produced the greatest transfer of

---

10. Countries like the UK, New Zealand and Australia had strict lockdowns and mandatory enforced vaccinations. States like Florida, Sweden, Uruguay, Iceland and Thailand all avoided long lockdowns and did not enforce vaccination. All of them reported low "excess deaths" during 2020-2022 and no "surge" of cases upon re-opening. This is astounding considering Florida, for one, is a state of senior citizens who were supposed to be at high risk of fatality due to COVID-19. They were old and enjoyed freedom—why didn't they die more than people in strict lockdown states that forced vaccination? Could the vaccines themselves be the cause of increased heart attacks, compromised immunity, and early death? To state-controlled media, this remains a mystery they choose not to investigate.

11. https://www.sciencedirect.com/science/article/pii/S0264410X24001919

wealth from the poor to the rich in human history. Oxfam recorded **573 new billionaires** due to wealth accumulation in Big Tech, Big Pharma and Transport Logistics. Many of those new billionaires directly profited from pandemic-related industries. They got rich selling rushed vaccines, new test kits, vaccine packaging, masks, sanitizers and/or pop up clinics which littered our parking lots and cities.

- "Never let a good crisis go to waste" was their motto. The World Economic Forum announced on June 3rd, 2020, "Now is the time for a Great Reset."[12] Its founder Klaus Schwab had a book launch timed specifically for the pandemic; his *COVID-19: The Great Reset* was out by July 9th, 2020. The following elites used the same phrase "Build Back Better" simultaneously to push for Klaus' vision of "Stakeholder Capitalism":
    - UN Secretary General António Guterres,
    - U.S. President Joe Biden,
    - U.K. Prime Minister Boris Johnson,
    - N.Z. Prime Minister Jacinda Ardern,
    - E.U. President Ursula von der Leyen,
    - French President Emmanuel Macron,
    - WHO Director Tedros Ghebreyesus, and of course, WEF founder Klaus Schwab.
- Dictators such as New Zealand Prime Minister Jacinta Ardern and Victorian Premier Dan Andrews became Big Pharma and China's marketing agents, rather than their constituent's' servants.
- For them and their cronies, the pandemic was a good time they wished would never end.
- Grudgingly the politicians had to let go of their

---

12. https://www.weforum.org/agenda/2020/06/now-is-the-time-for-a-great-reset/

heavy-handed bludgeon of unconstitutional powers. Most countries have forgotten how dishonest and harmful these politicians were.
  - God wanted us to know about the pandemic beforehand because it triggered the White Horse of the Apocalypse. (Yes, we will cover all the common objections Christians have. They're easy to answer.)

- Predict that civil unrest or war on the streets would break out in June 2023. This was fulfilled in the French riots of June 2023, to be discussed in detail later as France has been the key to several historic events. I posted a video about the fulfillment in July 2023, titled **"PROPHECY of NEXT 10 YEARS: France Triggers the Red Horse."**

Prophecy of Next 10 Years

- Predict the October 7 Attacks on Israel by Hamas **9 years before it happened** (2016), and then again **1 day before it happened** (October 6, 2023). Based on a Jewish boy's vision of WW3, I warned the world that the IDF would be taken by surprise, Israelis would be taken hostage, and this would be one of the most significant end time signs leading to the revelation of the Anti-Christ—the last part is yet to occur (at the time of my writing). He's alive even now and his plan to seize control is already in motion.

9 years before it happened

- Predict the exact locations where at least 3 disasters will fall on America as signs of judgment. I call them **"America's Final Warnings."** They are marked out by the path of the 3 Great American Solar Eclipses.[13]

    1 day before it happened

    - The first was in Houston, fulfilled by Hurricane Harvey on August 25-29, 2017. I stood in the city of Houston to give this prophetic warning days before it happened. Many Texans were in the service with me and recall it. The church where I stood was flooded and could not be used. Pastor Joel Osteen's megachurch Lakewood was flooded and faced criticism for not immediately helping provide supplies and shelter for evacuees. At that time, it was the costliest natural disaster in US history.
    - The second judgment was fulfilled in Kerrville, another town in Texas. I was invited to watch the third and last Great American Solar Eclipse on April 8, 2024 at Kerrville. The family of Max Greiner invited me to celebrate at his property where he erected a landmark 77-foot-7-inches tall steel sculpture of **"The Empty Cross."** Believe it or not, that is the epicenter of the intersection of the two solar eclipses that crossed the continental United States in 2023 and 2024. "X" truly marked the spot! Due to the anticipated congestion in Kerrville, I decided our family should watch the eclipse at our friends' place in McKinney. I had a soft spot for this little town and when the eclipse neared totality on

---

13. 21 August 2017, 14 October 2023, and 8 April 2024.

that cloudy day, the skies parted, the animals stilled, the temperature dropped and we experienced the eclipse in its full glory—what a sign of God!

- I posted several videos on YouTube and Rumble before the event explaining its prophetic meaning: "**APRIL 8 ECLIPSE**" and "**TERROR Eclipses | What No one Told You About…the Sign of Jonah**."

| April 8 Eclipse

- There was also a follow up post on YouTube addressing objections to "**It's NOT the Sign of JONAH!**" Although I issued the warning of the intersection being centered on Kerrville (I was not the only one who noticed the geography in 2024), I did not think Kerrville would ever make international news. One year and 88 days later, on July 4th, 2025, a bizarre flash flood carried away 27 Christian campers and counselors in the wee hours of the morning (4-5am) at Camp Mystic in Kerr County. I personally heard of one Christian girl who wanted to attend this very camp and her father forbade her. She was disappointed at first, but she obeyed. How thankful the family must be now that their girl listened to authority. This is not to blame those

| TERROR Eclipses

| It's NOT the Sign of JONAH!

Christians who attended, but to point out that God is not unfair. He always warns though we do not always listen. Christians who die are in a much better place and we honor their memory by remembering they are a sign for us. **1 Peter 4:17** says, *"For it is time for judgment to begin at the household of God; and if it begins with us, what will be the outcome for those who do not obey the gospel of God?"* They went first and they went to a better place.

- Predict the day Joe Biden would drop out of the 2024 Presidential race, to the very day, even though he had vowed not to drop out. I believe he sincerely didn't know he would drop out. He was forced by an internal coup to relinquish his presumptive nomination in favor of VP Kamala Harris, who was underqualified for the campaign and the job. This was posted in my video **"BIDEN About to be REPLACED"** on July 18, 2024; followed up by **"BIDEN GONE! 15 Years of PROPHECIES Fulfilled."**

BIDEN About to be REPLACED

BIDEN GONE! 15 Years of PROPHECIES Fulfilled

- Two strange things preceded Biden's removal from the race. First, the White House said he was diagnosed with COVID. The vaccines he advocated for did nothing to stop transmission. Secondly, the Democratic National Convention (DNC) refused to ratify, and then delayed ratifying his nomination as the candidate for the Democrats. No incumbent U.S. president eligible for re-election has ever lost their party's nomination in a primary contest. The modern primary system of the 20th century gives incumbent presidents significant advantages: name recognition, party loyalty, fundraising power, and control over the party machinery.

- Yet, as predicted, Biden announced his dropout on Sunday July 21, 2024. I predicted July 20—I was off by 13 hours. Sunday was an unusual day for the White House to make such announcements. Perhaps the decision *was* made on Saturday and his team decided to make it public on Sunday. Ten minutes later Biden followed up his tweet with a grudging endorsement of Kamala Harris—the soon-to-fail Democrat nominee.

- Predict **a major attack on American soil before September 11, 2025**. This was fulfilled on September 10, 2025, by the public assassination of Charlie Kirk (1993-2025). This was the first Christian martyrdom in America most people saw (people heard of one in 1968, when Martin Luther King Jr. was shot in the jaw and neck, but it was not televised). Kirk was a notable Christian speaker, conservative influencer, and founder of Turning Point USA (2012). His death has sparked a global awareness of Christianity and conservatism. Young people watched and re-watched his videos. His funeral was attended by the President, Vice President, Secretary of State, Secretary of Defense, FBI Director, nearly all cabinet members, and the "Who's Who" of America's Right. It was viewed by over 100 million people. To put that in perspective, Queen Elizabeth II's funeral in 2022, a time when everybody was at home under COVID lockdowns, received only 28 million views in the UK and USA.

- My video prediction was titled "**Is America READY for the Next 9/11?**" I truly did not know it would be Charlie Kirk. I was glad it was not a mass casualty attack. Only one person died to trigger a seismic spiritual shift. All the Lord told me was that it would happen before September 11.

Is America READY for the Next 9/11? (Before Sep 11, 2025)

I've been pastoring for 25 years. You learn a lot being on the same job for that long. You learn how much you weren't ready for the job. You learn how much you weren't taught and should have been taught in Bible school. You learn that the Lord uses us despite our failings and ignorance, so long as we stay humble enough to continue to be discipled—which means to never stop learning. You learn the Lord works far beyond our human knowledge. He is creating a cosmic drama out of the lives of those who choose to obey Him. Here are two examples.

Our church started on *Yom Teruah* (the Feast of Trumpets) in 2000. For those who don't know, that's the next prophetic feast waiting to be fulfilled. For many prophecy watchers, it represents the day "the trumpet will sound, and the dead will be raised imperishable, and we shall be changed."[14] Did I know it was a prophetic day on God's Calendar when I planted the church in Melbourne, Australia? No. I was simply obeying the Lord as promptly as I could organize a location and a team. Our start was prophetic and pointed to this book you're holding! It led us here.

Recently we celebrated our Silver Anniversary on *Yom Kippur* (the Day of Atonement) in 2025. It happened to correspond to the highest, holiest day on the Jewish calendar. Did I plan that? No. Only one week before we celebrated, I looked at the calendar and

---

14. 1 Corinthians 15:52

realized, *"How nice of God! He marked our church anniversary on His holy calendar: 1 October 2025 equals 10 Tishri 5786."*

This holiday points to the day that one third of the Jews will be humbled and will call upon Yeshua as their own Messiah.[15] When the Anti-Christ (better named the Anti-Semite) turns on the Jews, and the whole world abandons the nation of Israel, then many millions of Jews will cry out in repentance (*teshuvah*) and ask God to forgive their sins.

I wasn't taught the Biblical holidays or the Hebrew calendar in Bible school. End Times is usually the weakest subject in any theological seminary. I know because I attended one of the best, and I've taught in several schools. I rub shoulders with professors who teach very little about the Book of Revelation that is definitive. They tell their students five theories and let the students pick their view. No other subject of the Bible is taught this way to ministers-in-training. We would not teach five theories about salvation and

---

15. **Isaiah 62:11** ...Say to the daughter of Zion, "Behold, your salvation [literally 'your *Yeshua*'] comes; behold, his reward is with him, and his recompense before him."

Zechariah 12:10 And I will pour out on the house of David and the inhabitants of Jerusalem a spirit of grace and pleas for mercy, so that, when they look on me, on him whom they have pierced, they shall mourn for him, as one mourns for an only child, and weep bitterly over him, as one weeps over a firstborn.

Zechariah 13:6 And if one asks him, 'What are these wounds on your back?' he will say, 'The wounds I received in the house of my friends.'

Zechariah 13:8-10 In the whole land, declares the Lord, two thirds shall be cut off and perish, and one third shall be left alive. 9 And I will put this third into the fire, and refine them as one refines silver, and test them as gold is tested. They will call upon my name, and I will answer them. I will say, 'They are my people'; and they will say, 'The Lord is my God.'"

Romans 9:27 And Isaiah cries out concerning Israel: "Though the number of the sons of Israel be as the sand of the sea, only a remnant of them will be saved,

Romans 11:25–26 Lest you be wise in your own sight, I do not want you to be unaware of this mystery, brothers: a partial hardening has come upon Israel, until the fullness of the Gentiles has come in. And in this way all Israel will be saved, as it is written, 'The Deliverer will come from Zion, he will banish ungodliness from Jacob.'

pray the Christian students pick one that suits them. That would be tantamount to spreading heresy. Lord forbid!

Yet we treat the Book of Revelation and God's Timeline this way. We no longer can afford this theological luxury (and confusion). Nearly everything in the Book of Revelation is understandable now. We have a lot to unpack, as academics are fond of telling students.

> Ramble Republic: I am a devout Christian and have been for a long time. But I always take prophecy, especially when it does not come straight from the Bible, with a big grain of salt. I remember just after your channel had made the prediction about Trump's assassination attempt, you had a special [video] several weeks later on just this. You believed that the intersection of the solar eclipses would bring some sort of travesty. I did not think much of it at the time, in fact, I doubted it quite a bit. This [Kerrville Flash Flood that killed 135 people in central Texas on July 4th, 2025] is very interesting. Thank you for doing the Lord's work as you have been called to do it.

CHAPTER 4
THE BIBLE IN ONE MINUTE

PEOPLE WHO DON'T READ the Bible have fallen way behind, because its prophecies are already coming to pass. Revelation is the last book of the Bible. It parallels Genesis. That is, Genesis and Revelation are very similar. Revelation reverses Genesis, so without it, the Bible would not be complete.

Genesis is a record of the only eye witness of our origins. It starts out with a perfect world created for a perfect pair of human beings: Adam and Eve. They had control of the whole world, but they sinned against God and their world fell under the consequences of sin, which include the curses of sickness, poverty, broken family, tyranny, injustice, and finally death. None of these curses were a part of God's perfect will for humanity. We brought pain on each other and on ourselves. God has never started a single war or broken a single home. We do that.

We also brought pain to God. God trusted us and we broke His trust. God *permitted* the freedom for us to do this, but He did not *commit* it. There's a world of difference between permission and commission. Because God's perfect will for humanity did not change, He revealed to Adam and Eve a 2-step plan to remedy the pain, suffering and injustices:

1) He would personally come to save whoever wanted the chance to be redeemed from sin—this promised Savior is also known as the Messiah. The surprise of prophetic literature is that He turns out to be none other than God the Creator Himself!

2) The Messiah would bring justice to victory, and destroy evil forever (Isaiah 42:1-4, Matthew 12:18-20).

> **Matthew 12:18-20**
>
> **"Behold, my servant whom I have chosen, my beloved with whom my soul is well pleased, I will put my Spirit upon him, and he will proclaim JUSTICE to the Gentiles. 19 He will not quarrel or cry aloud, nor will anyone hear his voice in the streets; 20 a bruised reed he will not break, and a smoldering wick he will not quench, until he brings JUSTICE to victory;**

This plan was revealed in Genesis. It began to be fulfilled by Jesus Christ in the New Testament. By the last two chapters of Revelation, everything returns to peace and perfection.

In between the beginning of Genesis and the end of Revelation, God gives us *prophecies* and *signs* so we who have eyes to see can know where we stand on **God's Timeline**.

Before the Great Day of Justice arrives, the Book of Revelation tells us of signs leading to the event. **Signs** are indicators of what's going to happen before the End. There are 22 of them: 22 major signs written in 22 chapters of the Book of Revelation. The Bible tells us, *"When you see these things, the End will be soon."*

> **Matthew 24:34**
>
> Truly, I say to you, this generation will not pass away until all these things take place.

The most famous signs out of the 22 are Seals 1, 2, 3, and 4.

Every Christian knows them. Even secular people who have never read the Bible have heard of the "4 Horsemen of the Apocalypse."

What are they?

1. The **White** Horse
2. The **Red** Horse
3. The **Black** Horse
4. The **Green** Horse

In English, the translators sometimes described the last horse as "pale." But the original Greek says "chloros," which is the root from which we get the word "chlorophyll," the chemical that makes plants green. So the last horse is green. Some English translations say "pale green."

Now you have a summary of the Bible in one minute. Whenever you read the Bible and it doesn't make sense in your own language, it's helpful to look up what the original language Greek or Hebrew says.

Let's now focus on the structure of the Book of Revelation.

CHAPTER 5
INTRODUCING THE BOOK OF REVELATION

GOD'S TIMELINE in 22 Chapters

If you don't know anything about the Book of Revelation, congratulations, you're about to become like a semi-pro. You're going to understand it better than most people out there, even better than many Christians. So here we go!

Revelation is the final book of the New Testament. Clearly, it's about the End Time—the last days. Its main subject is Jesus, as the first verse says, "The Revelation of Jesus Christ" (1:1). Revelation is always singular, though some people misquote it as "revelations."

The English word "**Revelation**" was translated from the Greek word "**Apocalypse**" (*apo*, "away" + *kalypto*, "cover") meaning disclosure, uncovering, or revealing. So the two words should be synonymous. When I named my church "Discover Church," little did I know at the time that in Latin, Greek, and Hebrew, my church would be named "Revelation Church." "Discover" comes from Latin *discooperire* (*dis*, "away" + *cooperire*, "to cover".)

Apocalypse should be as positive a word as Discover. It does not mean catastrophe, doom, or hidden. It means the opposite: "To reveal, to uncover, to discover." But due to ignorance, the secular world has put a negative spin on the word apocalypse.

Revelation predicts 2000 years of Church history in only two chapters (2-3). It spends a disproportionate amount of content on the worst 7 years on earth. No period of time receives more signs, more warnings, or more attention in prophetic literature than these 7 years. Theologians call it the Tribulation.

Tribulation comes from the Latin threshing tool *tribulum*, a heavy, flat sledge (smooth on one side, rough on the underside) that is dragged over the harvest, crushing the stalks on the threshing floor to release the grain. The *tribulum* separates the wheat from the chaff, the grain from the husk. For this reason, tribulation came to mean "severe trouble, trials, distress, suffering, or adversity."[1] The Tribulation is the worst 7 years on Earth, but it ends with Jesus' return, His triumph over satan, our victory over death, the start of the new Millennium, and a bright future for all eternity.

When God gave Revelation to the Apostle John (the last survivor of the 12 Apostles), he didn't write it in chapters, but we believe even the division of the Bible into chapters and verses was foreordained. God knew about it and He put significance and meaning into it.

The Book of Revelation has 22 chapters, and it's basically a timeline. If you read it like a timeline, it's like watching a movie from start to finish.

---

1. It is prophetic that Jebus/Jerusalem comes from a Canaanite root meaning "threshing floor" (Joshua 18:28). The *"salem"* that was added means "peace." After the threshing separates the unbelievers from the believers, then there will come peace. The Temple Mount itself was a threshing floor before David bought it (2 Samuel 24:18-25, 1 Chronicles 21:18-25). It's supernatural that this city that has no waterway is the center of global conflict and world news. The prophet Zechariah said, "Behold, I will make Jerusalem a cup of trembling unto all the people round about, when they shall be in the siege both against Judah and against Jerusalem." (12:2) The threshing continues in Jerusalem, true to its name.

SCENE SHIFTS IN THE STORYLINE

The reason people sometimes become confused is that Revelation is like most movies. You're not going to stay on one person, or in one room the whole movie. There are scene shifts. This is what happens in the Book of Revelation. God is a good narrator, better than Hollywood.

Chapters 1–22 are a chronology. They are God's timeline for the end times. However…

Chapters 4 and 5, and 14 and 15 are scene shifts where God wants to show us what's happening in Heaven. So, we're seeing what's happening in Heaven, which means from Earth's perspective, the end of Chapter 3 connects with the beginning of Chapter 6.

Because people don't realize these scene shifts, they get confused and tend to think a lot of time has passed between chapters 3 and 6. No! Chapters 3 and 6 are right next to each other in time. In plain English, the end of the Church Age (3) and the opening of the Seals of Revelation (6) are in the same timeframe.

The same is true with Chapters 13 and 16. Since God takes believers away to Heaven in Chapters 14 and 15, from Earth's perspective Chapters 13 and 16 are right next to each other. It's that easy. God's not trying to confuse us.

Revelation 1-7 describe the Church Age, a 2,000-year timeline that is based on the characteristics of the 7 churches in Asia (present-day Turkey).

Revelation 6-8:5 are the **7 Seals** or Pre-Tribulation Events.

Revelation 8:6-10 are the **7 Trumpets** or Tribulation Events.

Revelation 11-13 are the **Mid-Tribulation** events, including synopses of the 2 Witnesses' ministry, the Dragon's persecution, Israel's protection, and the two Anti-Christs (aka the Beast and his False Prophet). This is when the Abomination of Desolation occurs, as it precedes the Jews fleeing Jerusalem. Jesus gives this sign as the final warning to His people the Jews. When they see the desecration of the Temple, they are to immediately flee for safety.

Revelation 16-18 are the **7 Bowls** or Great Tribulation Events. The 7th bowl, the destruction of Mystery Babylon, is so critical that two whole chapters (17 and 18) are devoted to it.

Revelation 19 is the Second Coming of Christ and the defeat of the world's Anti-Christs and their systems of oppression and deception.

Revelation 20 is the incarceration of Satan and the start of the New Millennium. This is 1000 years of Christ ruling with the "called and chosen" on earth. It's a practice run. This is the final training for those who will be counted worthy to rule with God in Eternity. It ends with a world war (20:7) and the Great White Throne Judgment (20:11).

Revelation 21-22 are about **Future Eternity**.

After 2,000 years of Church and 1,000 years of the Millennial Reign of Christ, we head into Eternity. We're basically in Earth school; we haven't begun real living yet. God has not shown us all the things He wants us to see and enjoy. We're just being trained; that's all this life is.

We the Church are in school right now. God has told us that at the end of this age, we will still not be ready. So He's going to add another 1,000 years. We're going to learn even more in that period of time—but that's for another day. Let's focus on the time we're living in now.

> Tracer: Great insight… Thank you Pastor Steve for your calm tone while discussing matters of the world. Lots of craziness happening & i just appreciate hearing your voice. Its very calming. May God continue to keep you & your family protected & clarity on the upcoming events

SUMMARY OF THE 22 JUDGMENTS

- **7 Seals** = 7 pre-Tribulation signs for the Church
- **7 Shofars** = 7 Tribulation events for the Jews
- **Mid-Trib** = 1 continuous event from the rise of the Anti-Christ, the desecration of the Temple, to the protection of the Jews in the "wilderness"
- **7 Bowls** = 7 Great Tribulation events for the Muslims, notably the 7th Bowl is the destruction of Babylon (Muslim territory) and the Anti-Semite Anti-Christ (a Muslim).
- <u>7 + 7 + 1 + 7</u> =
- **22 Signs** of the End Times

TWO COMMON MISCONCEPTIONS ABOUT REVELATION 6

Since Chapters 2 and 3 are a summary of the 7 churches of Asia Minor, and Chapter 4 has a voice calling John to "come up hither," many people assume the Rapture happens at Chapter 4, and we're not going to be here at Chapter 6.

These are assumptions people have turned into doctrine. But we should never base doctrine on one single verse or, in this case, only 3 words from one verse.

Another assumption is that Chapter 6 is equivalent to the start of the Tribulation. So let's ask the questions: What does the text actually say? Will we still be here in Chapter 6? Will the Tribulation start in Chapter 6? Let the Word speak for itself. You'll see how to clear up these questions in the next chapter. We are about to, so to speak, open the seals.

CHAPTER 6
WHEN DO THE 7 SEALS OPEN?

THE 22 EVENTS predicted in Revelation are symbolized by 7 seals, 7 trumpets, 1 Mid-Tribulation Abomination, and 7 bowls. The events are triggered by the opening of the first seal, which is clearly defined as a global event.

Seals are not commonly used today, except on some official documents and graduation certificates. In ancient times, seals were not stickers or stamps. Seals were made of melted wax that was imprinted with a personal ring; as it dried it closed shut a scroll. The seal prevented tampering and signified legal authority (e.g. royal seals on decrees, personal seals on contracts).

The word "seal" in all its variants occurs 58 times in the ESV. You may recognize 58 is the number of Noah and the end times. (See my book *The Divine Code: A Prophetic Encyclopedia of Numbers, Volume II* for an explanation of 58.) Modern courts still use the term "sealed" document to mean "confidential,"  even though it no longer uses wax. To "seal" a document means to hide it from the public temporarily, often to protect sensitive information such as private data, trade secrets, or national secrets. The important point is that sealing doesn't destroy or erase the document, it just controls disclosure. For instance, adoption records stay sealed until the child turns 18, then can be opened upon request.

This is what happens in Revelation 5 when we are introduced to a book in the right hand of God, sealed with 7 seals. A "strong angel" in Heaven proclaims with a loud voice, "Who is worthy to open the scroll and break its seals?" (5:2) A request is being made for someone to open the 7 seals that temporarily hide the content of this book. John so strongly desires to read this book he weeps that no one is qualified to open the seals, until Jesus walks up to God the Father and takes the book out of His hand (5:7). The seals can be broken by the right person at the right time—the time of disclosure, the time of revelation.

The concept of a "seal" appears for the first time in Genesis 38 when Judah mistook his daughter-in-law Tamar for a prostitute, because she was veiled. She had been childless and bereaved of two husbands, Er and Onan, Judah's sons. Judah promised to give her his other son, but for fear he too would die, he kept him from her. She desperately wanted a baby.

Before they had sex, he promised to pay her a young goat (average price of US$500). She agreed on one condition: "If you give me a pledge...your signet and your cord and your staff." (38:17-18) This showed Judah carried his seal on him as a unique and important personal item, similar to how we carry our ID cards.

Judah agreed and she conceived twins (one of whom would become an ancestor of Messiah). When Judah found out Tamar was pregnant and he didn't know who the father was, he wanted to condemn her to death (38:24). To vindicate herself, she showed him his own signet, cord and staff. By this he was convicted that she was more righteous than he was.

A strange story of a crime that wasn't punished,[1] of a righteous person turning out to be the bad guy, and of a sinner turning out to be the good woman. I believe these themes run through the 7 seals of Revelation, too.[2]

The story of Judah's seal is our first clue that the 7 seals of Revelation are not when full blown justice or God's wrath will be revealed. The seal actually saves Tamar and her two babies. It had to be handed over and returned to save them all from death. The first 4 seals are particularly famous because their opening releases the 4 Horsemen of the Apocalypse. So we come to our question of today:

CAN THE 7 SEALS BE OPENING NOW?

Can the Horsemen of the Apocalypse be riding as we speak? There are two extreme positions that Christians currently hold:

1) **The 7 Seals *cannot* be opened because the Tribulation hasn't started.** The Tribulation hasn't started either because the Anti-Christ hasn't been revealed (the "white horse" of Revelation 6 is assumed to be the Anti-Christ), or because the Rapture hasn't happened yet (the phrase "Come up hither" spoken to John in Revelation 4 is inferred to mean the Church is to come up to Heaven or "rapture") and the Rapture must precede the first seal.

---

1. Incest and adultery were both punishable by death. Judah and Tamar both should have been stoned. Instead, they were blessed with two children, one of whom would be vital to the plan of Redemption.
2. There are a lot of clues about the future in this story of the seal. It includes a pregnancy/birth pangs (a picture of pre-Tribulation signs) and a delivery of two males, representing the two comings of Jesus—the first time He had a scarlet thread tied to his hand (in the form of His blood on the cross), the second time He will be fully revealed as Messiah to the Jews. Zerah came out first then withdrew. Perez then "breached" or "broke through." Who nearly killed the twin babies? Judah! Who saved the babies? The "daughter/wife," which can only represent the Church, who is both a daughter of the Jewish faith and an ignored woman courting the Jews to come back to God's will and produce fruit for God again.

2) **The Tribulation has already started because the seals have already opened.**

I regularly receive posts holding either one of these positions. People forward them to me because they want me to comment on them, whether I agree or disagree. Having examined them, I can see they're both wrong, surprisingly for the same reason.

They don't understand that the seals are *pre*-Tribulation signs. We know this 6 ways:

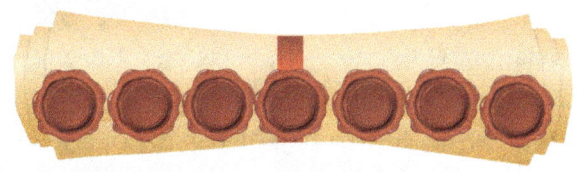

1) **The events of Revelation 6 match perfectly the birth pangs described by Jesus in Matthew 24 and Luke 21**. Birth pangs are pre-Tribulation signs. As Jesus said, when you see these things, "See that you are not troubled; for all these things must come to pass, but the end is NOT yet." (Matthew 24:6, my emphasis)

2) **The description of the seals in Revelation 6 matches reality**—what is happening now, not some theory about what might happen or who might be the Anti-Christ. I'll prove this to you in the Chapter "The White Horse."

3) **Revelation 6 ends by saying the wrath of God** (an idiom for the time of Tribulation) **had NOT yet come**. "And the kings of the earth, the great men, the rich men, the commanders, the mighty men, every slave and every free man, hid themselves in the caves and in the rocks of the mountains, and said to the mountains and rocks, "Fall on us and hide us from the face of Him who sits on the throne and from the WRATH of the Lamb! For the GREAT DAY of His WRATH has come, and who is able to stand?" (6:15-17

NKJV, my emphasis) In other words, prior to the opening of the 6th seal, the Tribulation had *not* yet begun!

4) **There is a lack of symmetry in the standard teaching of the Revelation timeline**. Popular prophecy preachers have assumed the 7 seals and 7 trumpets belong in the first half of Tribulation (3.5 years), and the 7 bowls fit in the second half of Tribulation (last 3.5 years). Where did we get this from? It's not from the text.

Why would God cram 14 events into 3.5 years, then 7 events into the last 3.5 years? It doesn't make sense. He made 3 sets of 7 signs in Revelation. Only the 7 trumpets and 7 bowls have a time stamp of 3.5 years, 42 months, or 1260 days.

Specifically, during the first half of Tribulation, Gentiles trample the holy city underfoot for 42 months (11:2) and the two witnesses prophesy for 1260 days (11:3) till they're killed and the world celebrates. This coincides with the rise of the Beast system and the acceptance of the Anti-Christ.

During the second half of Tribulation, the beast (Anti-Christ) is given authority for 42 months (13:5) and the Woman with 12 stars (Israel made up of 12 tribes) flees to the wilderness where she is protected by God for 1260 days (12:6).

The 7 trumpets fit into 3.5 years, the 7 bowls fit into 3.5 years, combining into 7 years that equal Daniel's 70th week or the time God deals with Israel. This makes the 7 trumpets and 7 bowls symmetric and the model elegant. It leaves us to deal with the 7 seals and figure out how long they last. *The most elegant solution is usually the right one.*

5) **The true meaning of "trumpets" has been missed because of English**. The word should be "shofars." Seven shofars signify God dealing uniquely with the Jews. That's the start of the 7 year period prophetically called Daniel's 70th Week (Daniel 9:27). Shofars are not Christian symbols. Shofars are Jewish musical instruments used in Jewish religious festivals and battles.

Here are some real comments I received from people who watch me on YouTube but have not studied the subject entirely (this is one reason this book is necessary... a few social media posts is not enough to explain end times to people):

> "If you believe the 4 horseman is [sic] already riding then you don't believe in pre tribulation rapture. There is some serious error going on with these teachings. I'm not being mean. But this is very disturbing because it is teaching false information. The book of Revelation is in order. Which means the snatching away comes before the 4 horseman" [sic = all spelling errors kept].

> "False doctrine. Rapture first then tribulation and 4 horses etc."

> "Im sorry, i had to shut it down at the 5 minute mark. You said the seals are opening, the first seal is open…however, that is not possible, we are still here, the church, the body of Christ, will not be here for the tribulation, it is not our message, we do not go through JACOBS trouble. Rapture FIRST, then tribulation THEN the coming of the Lord."

> "Wrath is after rapture, or we have been severely deceived so if there is not a rapture we are all in big trouble and under great deception. Misinterpreting the prophecies related to saving us from the wrath to come. So if the seals are being opened pre-trib show me that in scripture because I'm not seeing it."

> "So isn't it the birth pains and then the rapture of the church and then the red horse?"

We can summarize all these comments into Theory 1: **"The**

seals cannot be opened because the Tribulation hasn't started."

We can rephrase their combined questions this way: "Isn't the correct order a) Birth pangs, b) Rapture, c) Tribulation starting with, d) the white horse [the Anti-Christ[3]], e) red horse, etc.?

Here's my answer: Where in the Bible does it say the white horse is the Anti-Christ? It doesn't. It's an assumption. I will show you who the White Horse is in the next chapter.

Furthermore, where does the Bible say the rapture must precede the seals? It doesn't. It's extrapolated entirely from inference that God's saying to John to "come up hither" in Revelation 4 means the "rapture of the church."

I know this position well because I was taught it in Bible school. I taught it myself. It's been repeated over and over in prophecy books and by prophecy teachers. Yes, Revelation 4 could be suggestive of a Rapture, but in context of the timeline, it's a scene in Heaven. It tells us nothing about the timing of the event.

From Earth's perspective, the end of chapter 3 coincides with the beginning of chapter 6. The Church is still around for the birth pangs, even if she's not here for the Tribulation. The 4 Horsemen clearly ride before the Tribulation starts. The text says so; for they say after the seals have opened, "For the GREAT DAY of His

---

3. Some books or speakers even claim that this white horse is Christ, because there is another white horse Jesus rides on in Revelation 19. Obviously they are not the same: a) Jesus' robe is red, dipped in blood (19:13), presumably the rider of the white horse is also white (6:1); b) Jesus is followed by millions riding on white horses and dressed in white, the rider of the white horse is not accompanied by saints; c) Jesus is holding a two-edged sword, the rider of the white horse is holding a bow; d) Jesus is wearing many crowns, the rider of the white horse was "given" a crown, e) the timing of Revelation 6 is before the Tribulation, the timing of Revelation 19 is the end of Tribulation—this is why understanding timelines is crucial to understanding everything else in the Bible. Timelines help us to understand the Old Testament. Likewise the correct timeline helps us understand prophecies. As you will see in this book, we propose a third option: the rider of the White Horse is neither Christ (Rev 19), nor the Anti-Christ (Rev 13), but one of many anti-Christs opposing God and trying to harm humanity (Rev 6).

WRATH has come." (Revelation 6:17) The Tribulation will start after the seals. The trumpets and the bowls will occur during Tribulation. The seals cover the birth pangs or pre-Tribulation events.

Going back to our movie analogy: most movies follow a chronological timeline, but nearly every good movie will have some flashback, when the director changes the scene to focus on a character or explain an event. God is better than Hollywood. He did this in Revelation long before Hollywood.

For instance, Chapter 12 concentrates on Israel. It doesn't mean Israel didn't exist before Chapter 12, does it? Chapter 13 introduces the Anti-Christ. It doesn't mean the Anti-Christ didn't exist before Chapter 13, does it? The Anti-Christ has to be alive long before he's introduced, yet he's not mentioned before.

Likewise, Chapters 4 and 5 focus on Heaven, but it doesn't mean the Church on earth has ceased to exist. The Church is still present in Chapter 6. The Church is being persecuted in Chapter 6! Her martyrs cry out during the 5th seal and ask, "How long, O Lord, holy and true, until You judge and avenge our blood on those who dwell on the earth?" (6:10)

HOW DO WE KNOW THESE ARE CHRISTIANS AND NOT JEWS?

1) They "had been slain for the word of God." (6:9) Jews are not currently slain for teaching Torah to the world. Jews are persecuted for their economic success, for taking land, for building settlements, for paging operations, for asymmetric wars, for spying and assassinations. Christians don't do any of those things. Christians are the only group slain for teaching the Bible worldwide.

2) "Then a white robe was given to each of them." This is the white robe of salvation, given only to believers in Jesus Christ. Jews do not believe in Jesus. They will not repent and believe in their own Messiah *en masse* till the Second Coming, when they cry out for a Savior to rescue them.

3) They were told to rest until "the number of their fellow servants and their brethren, who would be killed as they were, was completed." (6:11). Jews are not referred to as "fellow servants" in the New Testament. The term means ministers of the Gospel. In Colossians, Paul called Epaphras "our dear fellow servant" (1:7) and Tychicus "a beloved brother and faithful minister, and fellow servant in the Lord" (4:7).

Who are these "martyrs for God's Word" if Christians have been raptured? It's no mystery. Christians have been martyred throughout the Church Age for 2000 years, and always for God's Word (translating it, preaching it, handing out Bibles where it's "illegal"). Christians will be persecuted during the pre-Tribulation 5th seal for preaching the Gospel and converting people from one religion to faith in Christ. Because Charlie Kirk preached that God made only two genders and marriage is only between a man and a woman, an angry man dating a transgender shot him. Kirk was "slain for the Word of God."

However, conditions change during the Tribulation: 1) Jews become the main target of persecution as the world turns against Israel and becomes more anti-Semitic, and 2) the main reason for executions during the Tribulation will be for "not accepting the mark of the beast."

Victims will include Jews, new Christians, libertarians, conscientious objectors, anti-government separatists and non-religious freedom fighters. They are not dying for "preaching the Word." The punishment will not be limited to Christians only.

Notice during COVID, when vaccination became a global "mark of approval," many types of people were persecuted, ostracized, and laid off their jobs. Christians were not the only group restricted or persecuted, though Bible-believing Christians tended to see the deception before others. Non-Bible-reading Christians were deceived and acted no differently than the world.

Another fan mail:

WHEN DO THE 7 SEALS OPEN?

> "WELL you are totally wrong on the pretrib rapture, what the 7 years covenant is, and who the antichrist is. YOU mean well but you are wrong."

No matter how many Scriptural reasons I present in this book, there will be a few believers who refuse to believe and grow spiritually. It's not a matter of "agreeing to disagree" when one side quotes the Bible and the other side ignores it. It's a case of willful ignorance. It's not putting God's Word first. I welcome objections when they are logically and consistently based on God's Word. But as the above comment suggests, it's emotional with no evidence from Scripture.

A moderator of an online group posted this, which I will call Theory 2:

- "I believe we're going to go through tribulation and great tribulation.
- October 5th, 2022 was the first seal was opened
- April 8th, 2023 was the second seal.
- October 11th and 12th (2024) was the third and fourth seals, and
- now the fifth seal was opened on October 2nd (2025).
- So the Lord has been opening the seals according to his calendar, the common rabbinic calendar or the Hillel calendar (referring to Hillel II who standardized the Jewish calendar in 359AD)....And so the 5th seal is opened. What is that seal? It's a, it's the, those who have been martyred for Christ... The meaning of this is we've entered into a season of great Christian persecution."[4]

She believes as I do that the seals have been opened, but she assumes that means the Tribulation has begun. We do not see

---

4. https://youtu.be/xkPpQQnlqc0?si=qj2OE4PSbdvpSF-S

conditions of the Tribulation at all. Her post is an illustration of **Theory 2: The Tribulation has already started because the seals have already opened.**

There are numerous errors here. This is clearly a case of "jumping the gun" because she doesn't know what the seals represent (the subject of the rest of this book), how they fit God's timeline (pre-Trib > Trib > Great Trib), and how they match reality. She seems to be a Sabbatarian and is committed to using only the Hebrew calendar to interpret the seals. She has selected *Yom Kippur* 2022 as the opening of the first seal, Passover 2023 as the second seal, *Yom Kippur* 2024 as the third and fourth seals (why two on the same day?), and *Yom Kippur* 2025 as the fifth seal. These dates have no evidence of any eschatological ties, and no ties to significant real world fulfillment.

As explained above, the seals can be opened and the Tribulation has not started yet. The text directly says so in 6:17.

SIXTH REASON THE 6 SEALS ARE PRE-TRIBULATION

6) When does the Rapture take place: before or after the seals? Since Revelation 4 precedes Revelation 6, isn't it obvious the Rapture happens before the seals? Let's follow this train of thought and agree "come up hither" can represent the Rapture of the Church. I believe God pre-empted the confusion and the wrong line of reasoning. All we have to do is read the text:

> **Revelation 4:1** (NKJV)
> After these things I looked, and behold, a door *standing* open in heaven. And the first voice which I heard *was* like a trumpet speaking with me, saying, "Come up here, and I will show you things which must take place after this."

I am convinced no detail in the Bible is there by accident.

Everything is by design. What's the curious phrase that is often ignored when Bible teachers explain chapter 4 verse 1? John said, "The voice which I heard was like a TRUMPET speaking with me."

By applying the #1 rule of Bible interpretation, Scripture interprets Scripture (*Sola Scripture*), we should correlate this trumpet with the first trumpet of Revelation 8. **The voice was "like a trumpet" because the Rapture happens around the first trumpet.** "Like" means approximation. I will be more precise about the timing later.

Suffice it to say, this phrase "like a trumpet" did not need to be there. But because Revelation 4:1 would be so misunderstood to mean an immediate escape of the Church before the birth pangs, God placed it there as an "easter egg" (a subtle clue or inside-joke that is not obvious at first, but rewards attentive watchers).

I've been teaching eschatology in churches and Bible schools for 24 years, since September 11, 2001.[5] I am familiar with the standard Pentecostal timeline and can present it like many Bible School teachers do. I am not challenging what is commonly taught. I am introducing a small adjustment to the timeline that will make the signs clear: the seals are the birth pangs—the signs *before* Tribulation.

---

5. That was one of the end time signs or divine warnings on America. America's final warning was given by the 3 solar eclipses crossing the continental United States from 2017-2024, forming 3 X's on the U.S. The first intersection has received judgment at least twice, both upon Texas (Hurricane Harvey, 25-29 August 2017 and the flash flood at Camp Mystic near Kerrville, 4 July 2025).

TRADITIONAL TIMELINE

Church Age >
Birth Pangs > (Rapture)[6] > **Tribulation = 7 Seals + 7 Trumpets**
> Mid-Tribulation > Great Tribulation = 7 Bowls >
Second Coming > Millennium > White Throne Judgment.

UPDATED TIMELINE

Church Age >
Birth Pangs = 7 Seals > (Rapture) > **Tribulation = 7 Shofars** >
Mid-Tribulation > Great Tribulation = 7 Bowls >
Second Coming > Millennium > White Throne Judgment.

This small modification helps both sides see they both can be right: the seals can be broken without the Tribulation starting. I base this refinement not only on the plain text, but also on revelation.

There is a well-accepted hermeneutical principle that the Bible is "progressive revelation." God reveals more to us as we progress in time, without contradicting what He revealed before. It seems to me non-controversial that we should know more now than theologians did 1000 years ago.

We can see the timeline of Revelation much clearer now than any time before. We are close to the Lord's coming. But people hang on to the old. Some Christians have theological or denominational

---

6. I put Rapture in parentheses because some believe it comes
   - before the Tribulation (called "Pre-Tribulation Rapture"),
   - during the middle of Tribulation ("Mid-Trib or Pre-Wrath Rapture"), or
   - after the Tribulation ("Post-Trib Rapture").

You can slide the Rapture around to suit your theory. God did not send me to argue over the timing of the Rapture. All 3 theories could be right as there seems to be multiple raptures. The Two Witnesses, for instance, get their own Rapture at Mid-Tribulation (11:1). It's not the focus or purpose of teaching End Times. Focus on what God focuses on: Justice! Increase justice on the Earth!

blinders on. Jesus described this inflexible mentality: "And no one puts NEW wine into old wineskins; or else the new wine bursts the wineskins, the wine is spilled, and the wineskins are ruined. But NEW wine must be put into NEW wineskins." (Mark 2:22 NKJV, my emphasis) Here's one subscriber who benefited from new wineskin:

> Brian B: Hi Steve and/or Staff member, I mainly just want to thank you for your ministry and teachings. I came across some youtube videos a couple weeks ago, and the were very educational, entertaining and encouraging.
>
> Since then, I've found calm and comfort listening to podcasts and youtube videos about the Bible.
>
> I've been particularly interested in end times teachings because I'm looking forward to Christ's return now more than ever. Pastor Steve's videos made more sense to me than most others I've watched and he helped resolve the conflict I was having between the pre-trib and mid-trib Rapture. I found both to have valid arguments and while I felt like Christians would live through the 7 seals, I also felt like Christians would be raptured before the full 7 year tribulation. Pastor Steve is the first one to suggest that both can be true, because the seals come before the rapture and before the tribulation.

I offer a 7th reason the seals come before the Tribulation in the chapter on Seals 5, 6 & 7.

CHAPTER 7
THE FLAGS

THE FIRST 4 SEALS, opened by the Lamb, release the "4 Horsemen of the Apocalypse." Who are they again? They are the riders on:

1. The **White** Horse
2. The **Red** Horse
3. The **Black** Horse
4. The **Green** Horse

These are the most famous word-pictures in the Bible. People who don't go to church know about the 4 Horsemen of the Apocalypse. Secular podcasters and non-Christians constantly use the term. After this chapter, you're going to find out what they're all about.

WHY THESE FOUR COLORS?

There is information contained in the colors. God is trying to reveal something to us. Do you believe that?

When it comes to Bible prophecy interpretation, you have to be patient. Some things you just cannot guess the meaning of until it's fulfilled. Let me ask you, what colors do you see in this flag?

THE FLAGS

What colors fly on the flag of the greatest enemy of Israel right now? They attacked and killed 1,200 civilians on October 7, 2023. They're called Palestinians. The colors on their flag happen to be the colors of the 4 Horsemen of the Apocalypse: white, red, black and green.

They claim that they have no nation of their own, but they do. Palestine was divided up into Jordan and Israel in 1922: Jordan (called the Emirate of Transjordan) got 77% of the land mass; Israel (called Palestine, but a homeland for Jews) was left with 23%. Jordan is the proper home of Palestinians.

The difference between the Jordanian and Palestinian flags is one star. They're nearly identical. When people have similar flags, it means they share similar heritage, similar ethnicity, similar history, similar language, similar food. They're the same people. That's why their flags look the same.

The flags of Australia and New Zealand differ by only one star. They share one of the world's closest bilateral relationships, often described as a "family" partnership, rooted in shared history, language, culture, and geography. Aussies and Kiwis have the privileges of visa-free entry, indefinite residence, and unrestricted work/study rights. They have a collective defense pact.

80 THE FOUR HORSEMEN OF THE APOCALYPSE

Australia, Fiji, New Zealand, Tuvalu and the United Kingdom all share "Union Jacks" on their flags. A Union Jack is a triple Christian symbol combining the crosses of St. George (England), St. Andrew (Scotland), and St. Patrick (Northern Ireland). 18 other British Overseas Territories (like Bermuda, Cayman Islands, Falkland Islands, Gibraltar, Jersey, etc.) also incorporate the Union Jack into their flags. Why would 23 sovereign countries and territories share the Union Jack? Because they share the same colonial heritage and/or are part of the British Commonwealth.

Let's look at the flag of Sudan. What colors do you see?

Sudan's flag looks almost identical to that of the Palestinians and Jordanians, only without a star. Sudan is a Muslim country that's predicted in Ezekiel 38 to join an anti-Semite coalition that will invade Israel in the end time.

THE FLAGS

Let's take a look at another Muslim country: **Kuwait**.

The country that started the Gulf War. Iraq invaded Kuwait in 1990 and started the Gulf War 1. I was in the United States for that. I was watching Operation Desert Shield (1990) and Operation Desert Storm (1991) live. That was the first time you could see bombs hitting foreign targets in real time. The U.S. was in Iraq again in Gulf War 2. Saddam Hussein was captured in 2003 and executed in 2006. Americans stayed in an 8-year war until 2011.

I wrote my first essay on Kuwait. I remember it well. How prophetic 40 years later I am still writing about this strategic nation!

How about the **United Arab Emirates** (UAE)? White, red, black, green.

How about **Libya**? Is it mere coincidence? All these Muslim nations have on their flags the colors of the 4 Horsemen of the Apocalypse: white, red, black and green.

Let's go to Afghanistan where Americans had war with the Taliban for 20 years (2001-2021). Afghanistan was the hideout of Osama bin Laden, the mastermind of the 9/11 attacks on the U.S. homeland.

What colors are on the flag of **Afghanistan**? You are becoming Bible prophecy experts! I call this Bible prophecy for non-Bible readers. Even a child gets it.

What colors are on the flag of **Syria**?

What colors are on the flag of **Iraq**? White, red, black and green.

Notice these two flags differ by only one star, just as those of Jordan and Palestine differ by only one star. What does it mean?

These territories have had overlapping borders, cultures, and history.

After World War I, the territories were divided by the 1916 Sykes-Picot Agreement between France and Britain. Syria fell under French mandate (until 1946), while Iraq was under British mandate (ending in 1932). The straight lines over the Middle Eastern desert were artificially drawn by Western powers. No country should have a straight line across vast amounts of land unless nobody lives there. We drew lines across Kurdish territory and other tribal people, separating families, tribes and Bedouins. We are the ones that caused those frictions.

This was why ISIS wanted to combine Syria and Iraq into the "Levant".[1] Its aim was to establish a revived caliphate under Abu Bakr al-Baghdadi.

President Donald Trump authorized airstrikes that killed Baghdadi on October 26, 2019, and terminated ISIS's top global leadership. Obama did little and let ISIS behead foreign workers, especially Christians in 2014-15. Trump effectively neutered ISIS during his first term.

Iraq and Syria have redesigned their flags post-Saddam (2008) and post-Assad (2024) respectively. Here's the new flag of Syria.

The new Syrian leadership are primarily former al-Qaeda members rebranded as nationalists. Even the new President

---

1. From the French word *lever* ("to rise"), referring to the "land where the sun rises" or the Eastern Mediterranean: Syria, Lebanon, Jordan, Iraq, Turkey, even Israel is included in this pan-Islamic dream.

changed his name from Abu Mohammed al-Jolani (a name on multiple international terrorist wanted lists) to Ahmed al-Sharaa.

What does the new Iraqi flag look like?

The Iraqi flag now features the *takbir* "*Allahu Akbar*" in green script at the center. Even the new designs, an attempt to reject the old regimes, maintain the 4 colors of the Horsemen of the Apocalypse! It's an enduring motif until the Second Coming.

Iran's flag is a little bit different from the rest. It's missing the 3rd color, black. Iran is different because they are Shia, whereas most Middle Eastern and North African countries are Sunni. Shia is a different branch of Islam, accounting for 10-15% of the global Muslim population. Even the difference is reflected in their flag.

Could all these colors matching the Book of Revelation be pure coincidence? Could you put any flag of any country into this prophecy? Well, no.

If you look at the flag of Russia, or Thailand, or Israel, or El Salvador, it would not fit Bible prophecy.

What if we compare the colors to the United States' flag? A lot of people think the United States is a bad actor in God's plan. Some claim Washington, D.C. is Babylon and a U.S. leader will be the

Anti-Christ. I don't believe so. I don't believe the United States is a bad actor, but I think the CIA runs a lot of the United States right now and that's not good—that's not the way it was intended to be. But the flag of the USA doesn't match the colors, neither do the flags of Ethiopia, India, Russia and Uruguay. You can just go down the family of nations and compare their flags.

The main players of World War 3 all share the same 4 colors for flags. It's very specifically the Arab Muslim nations. In other words, God already told us by simple colors, by an object lesson, the main players of World War 3. They can be recognized by these 4 colors on their flags—white, red, black, and green.

A SIMPLE ERROR

Bible prophecy teachers have misled Christians into assuming that whoever is the enemy of America must be the Anti-Christ, the enemy of God and Israel. God in His mercy raised up Pastor Steve as an outsider and sent him to America to awaken the Church.

Why didn't we see this before? Because Bible prophecy teachers have taught for over 50 years an American-centric doctrine. American culture has become the Gospel. Whoever is the enemy of America must be the Anti-Christ. As an example, for a long time Russia was America's enemy, so Gorbachev had to be the Anti-Christ. This is not the way to teach the Bible. This is why I'm sent from outside of America to tell Americans to go back to the Bible.

The Bible is a book for America but it's not an American book. So you cannot say, *"We hate Russia, therefore, the Anti-Christ will be Russian."* Look at it from the perspective of Israel. On March 21,

2024, Russia vetoed UN Resolution 220 that would have stopped Israel from crippling Hamas. Hamas was killing Jews and Christians. Russia stood up for Israel and Christians.

It's hard for Americans to admit that America constantly interferes in Israel's affairs and empowers her enemies. President Trump wanted the 2025 war with Iran to end as soon as possible; Israel wanted to finish the job. Israel was stopped from taking out Iran's top leadership. Trump wanted the 2023-25 war with Hamas to end as soon as possible and get a Nobel Peace Prize; Israel wanted to go into Gaza, rid it of every terrorist and rescue its hostages. On October 12, 2025, Trump got his wish, Israel relented, and a ceasefire with Hamas was announced. The world wants to show more mercy and compassion on terrorists (Hamas) than the victims (Israeli civilians and hostages).

Let me be clear: I celebrate the release of hostages held by Hamas for 738 days. Alongside this, Israel had to release 1,968 Palestinian prisoners, among whom 250 are convicted murderers and terrorists. They go free. They walk and some will kill again. The ceasefire only buys time for the terrorists to regroup and come back harder against Jews with bigger, better weapons.

Obama, on his way out of office, airlifted $1.7 billion in euros and Swiss francs on pallets to Iran. A parting gift for a regime that calls Israel "Little Satan" and America "The Great Satan." During his presidency, he sent $3.5-4 billion of "aid" to Palestinians via USAID and the Palestinian Authority (PA). DOGE, the Department of Government Efficiency led by Elon Musk, uncovered USAID as the primary front for unthinkable waste, absurd spending, and "irredeemable corruption."

Yet we think Russia is the Anti-Christ nation because American preachers told us so. Russia has a great relationship with Israel. One million Jews can speak Russian. Russians and Jews can travel to each other's countries for up to 90 days without a visa. They have a longstanding bilateral visa-free agreement. They have a military pact. As mentioned above, in 2024 Russia vetoed the UN Resolution to stop Israel from punishing Hamas. Russia also told Iran in 2025 it would not come to their rescue if President Trump were to bomb their nuclear facilities, and advised Iran to agree with Trump quickly.

Russia is a Christian nation that protects traditional values. Do you know Russia has had laws against "homosexual propaganda" since 2013? Does America have anything close? Does America export godly values or decadent immorality? Russia is actually standing for Israel and for Christians right now.

In some ways, Russia is defending Israel more than America is. How is it possible that Russia is going to invade Israel in the End Time? Where did this idea come from? This came from American prophecy teachers who disliked Russia and misapplied linguistics. They saw "*Rosh*" in Ezekiel 38:3 and 39:1 and said that sounded like the enemy they didn't like: "Russia."

"*Rosh*" means one thing: "Head," "Chief" or "Leader." It is translated "chief" in most English Bibles. It was left untranslated as "*Rosh*" in the NKJ, NASB and ESV. You cannot take a Hebrew word "*Rosh*" and turn it into an English name  "Russia." That makes no linguistic sense. It's a biased interpretation. But we in America did that, and we, as the Church accepted it over the years.

But now we can see the colors of 4 Horsemen of the Apocalypse are all common on Islamic flags. We see the main aggressors listed in Ezekiel 38 are today all Islamic: Turkey, Iran, Libya, Sudan.

Persia used to be a friend of Israel. Sudan used to have many Christians. Turkey used to be the global center of Christianity: Paul was born there, John lived there, Mary died there, all 7 Churches of Revelation are there.

The largest church in the world for 916 years, the *Hagia Sophia*, is in Istanbul. Today, that gem of Christianity has been converted into a mosque. Less than 1% of the population is Christian. 99% are Muslims. The 4 main players in Ezekiel 38-39 and the 4 colors of the horses of the Apocalypse share one thing in common: Islam.

Russia is a Christian nation. Russia borders Islamic regions and nations such as Chechnya, Azerbaijan, and Kazakhstan. She has had a long history of fighting Islamist terrorists (1999 Apartment Bombings, 2002 Moscow Theatre Crisis, 2004 Beslan School Siege, 2010 Moscow Metro Bombings, 2024 Moscow Concert Hall Shooting). America shouldn't be the enemy of Russia.

America couldn't have won World War 2 without Russia. More Russians died to defeat Nazis than Americans did. When America was attacked on September 11, Putin was the first world leader to call President Bush and offer aid. They don't consider us their enemy, but we keep pushing them. Sometimes good people snap. I pray for Putin not to snap.

If our end-time theology was better, or if we remembered our history better, we would have prayed better and harder for our ally in World War 2. Eschatology matters. May the revelation of the 4 colors encourage other Bible prophecy teachers to let the Bible speak in its time, and not insert our culture and assumptions into it, which twist the meaning of the Bible.

Pastor John Kilpatrick of Church of His Presence (CHP) and the Brownsville Revival (1995-2000), sent me this text:

> Pastor John Kilpatrick: I remember your messages [at CHP on the 4 Horsemen]. Loved them…you shared such revelation. I love the way that you shared the flags. Unforgettable. You have a very unique preaching style that sets you apart from others.

CHAPTER 8
THE WHITE HORSE

1ST SEAL: **The White Horse**

> **Revelation 6:1-2** (NKJV)
> **1** Now I saw when the Lamb opened one of the seals; and I heard one of the four living creatures saying with a voice like thunder, "Come and see."
> **2** And I looked, and behold, a white horse. He who sat on it had a bow; and a crown was given to him, and he went out conquering and to conquer.

If you read this any time before 2020, there was no way you could guess the meaning. Some said it's Christ coming on a white horse. Some said it's the Anti-Christ coming on a white horse. You couldn't get more opposite interpretations. This is a genuine problem for Bible teachers: they're assigned to teach a subject and when they don't know it, they often resort to guesswork. They act like they know when they are only speculating.

I try very hard not to guess. I try to let the Bible speak to me and not insert my culture and my assumptions into it. Once we start inserting our presumptions, we twist the meaning of it.

After hearing prophecy teachers guess the meaning of the white horse rider for 30 years, I said to myself, "You know what? I've preached this passage for years, and I don't know what the crown or the bow represents. I can see other teachers don't know yet either. I will wait on the LORD to reveal it to me."

Then He did! John the Baptist said, "A man can receive nothing, except it be given him from heaven." (John 3:27 KJV) Jesus said to Peter, "For flesh and blood has not revealed this to you, but my Father who is in heaven." (Matthew 16:17) Paul said when he did not receive the approval of Christians who were suspicious of him, "For I did not receive it from any man, nor was I taught it, but I received it through a revelation of Jesus Christ." (Galatians 1:12)

I never heard of any other man preaching what I'm about to tell you before I did. The Lord showed it to me and everywhere I share it, it's an eye-opener. Once you hear it, you'll never forget it.

The Lord is constantly shedding new light on old Scriptures. One way to receive more from Him is to work through the non-Biblical assumptions we hold. An assumption I heard for years from prophecy preachers was that the rider on the White Horse had a bow, but not any arrows. I heard it for three decades, "Well, this horse has a bow, but he doesn't have an arrow. He's an arrowless, bow-carrying Anti-Christ. He's not that powerful." You can make up all sorts of pictures, preach up a storm and get people excited, but the truth is, that's wrong.

Here's a comment from social media expressing a variation of this view:

> The rider on the white horse is the antichrist. He receives a bow, it's symbolic of power and authority. We see the rider on the white horse is the only one that receives a crown. We have seen that May 6th of this year (2023). Believe me, pray and do your research. It's King Charles and he is here and ready.

Nothing in the text says the white horse equals Christ or the Anti-Christ. Nothing in the text says he has a bow but no arrows. These are all made-up assumptions. Stick to the text.

Let's say you hear me shout in a crowded theater, "Everybody, watch out! There's a man with a gun over there!" And you stand up in the middle of the crowd and say, "Oh, no worries. Pastor Steve didn't say there's a gun with bullets. He only said there's a gun. He didn't say bullets."

You're going to be the first guy shot dead. That's stupid.

If someone said in ancient times, "That rider is armed with a bow! He's got a bow!" you wouldn't nonchalantly say, "Hey, don't worry about it. He didn't mention that he has arrows."

What?! The arrows come with the bow! It's a package. You don't need to say it.

Let's go through the 3 clues we're given from the text.

WHITE

Who wears white today? Since the rider goes forth to conquer the whole world, the color white should be universally recognized. I can think of a few things white universally represents:

- Purity
- A wedding dress
- The medical/pharmaceutical industry

I'm sure the Lord is not telling us to look for a newly married bride to be riding on a white horse and conquering the whole world. Her interest would only be in her new husband.

I'm also sure the Lord is not calling a man with a bow conquering the whole world pure. He's not related to purity.

White is the color of the pharmaceutical/medical profession. Most doctors and pharmacists I meet wear white lab coats. When I moved to America, one thing I noticed right away was how many pharmaceutical ads were on TV. Americans watch more commercials for drugs than any other country I've lived in. Everybody seems to be sick and so many ads are about drugs. I also noticed when the actors or actresses would come on TV, they had to dress in white lab coats, as though wearing white gave them more credibility.

White seemed to be the universal symbol of the pharmaceutical industry. So, I tucked that in my mind and said, "Okay, I'm going to watch out for something like that because I don't know any other commonly seen white right now."

HORSE

Why a horse? Why not hippos or monkeys? God could have picked a lion. It's not a lion. God picked an animal that is domesticated and controlled by a horseman. In other words, the things that will be unleashed by the opening of the seals are going to be man-made. They're not natural catastrophes.

A horse is a domesticated animal that is controlled by a horseman. Something is being engineered and steered by a man.

BOW AND ARROWS

Even though only the bow is mentioned, I can prove to you the bow and arrows come as a set. The Greek word translated "bow" is "*toxon*" (τόξον). You're going to recognize this word, because in English we derive the words "toxic," "toxicology," and "intoxication" from it.

Why would we derive the word "toxic" from the Greek word "toxon"? Because in ancient times when they fought each other, they realized it's not easy to kill someone. When someone is hit with an arrow, they don't always die. It's not like in the movies. They kick a person once, they fall down and don't get up again. They shoot someone once and they die right away. Perhaps one bullet to the head will do that. But an arrow is not going to necessarily kill a person if it hits the wrong spot.

People are not easy to kill. I once witnessed to a woman and she didn't accept Christ. Later her husband stabbed her over 40 times and she still lived. He was sent to jail and she was traumatized forever. I believe the Lord tried to reach her before tragedy struck, but she rejected it. The Lord doesn't cause pain. People cause pain on each other. The Lord sends warnings and ways out, then He lets you choose.

So ancient armies learned to be efficient. They didn't want to waste arrows during war. They learned that if they dipped the arrow in *toxon* (poison), then when they shot the enemy, the victim died faster. It was the poison that killed them. Hence, the whole package, the entire weaponry was called the *toxon* because it delivered the poison through a sharp needle.

CROWN

So far, the Bible is telling us somebody wearing white is going to deliver something sharp into your skin and it will transmit a toxin into your body. If we still don't know what this is about, God foretold this person is going to be given a "crown."

I was preaching in El Salvador and Honduras in 2024. We read Revelation 6:2 everywhere I went. In one meeting, I said to a group of 70 Spanish-speaking pastors, "Would you please read that again? What is the White Horse given?"

And they said, "Una corona."

I said, "Can you say that again?"

They said, "Una corona."

I asked, "What was the pandemic sparked by? What virus?"

All the people's jaws dropped. I was teaching pastors and none of them had seen it before I said it. The pandemic was over and they had not connected the "crown" of the White Horseman to the coronavirus pandemic. It was right in front of their eyes in the

Spanish Bible. They were suddenly excited by prophecy! Prophecy is for Latin America. Prophecy is for now.

We who read the Bible in English have a slight disadvantage. We don't see some things right away, at least not as fast as people who read other European languages. In most Romance languages, the meaning should be obvious. The Latin word for crown is *corona*. In Spanish, Italian, Romanian, Catalan, Sardinian, and even Maltese, the word for crown is *corona*.[1] Why did it take a non-Spanish speaker to show Spanish preachers the meaning of their Spanish Bible?

You can read the Bible like your eyes are blinded. Until it happens, until the prophecy is manifested, you don't know what it's about. Do you know what that proves? That God wrote the Bible!

The prophets did not always understand what they were inspired to pen. Pastors do not always understand what they're assigned to teach the flock. We need God's help! Our eyes seem to be blinded until the prophecy is fulfilled.

The Bible tells us a man dressed in white is going to come with something sharp that's dipped in poison and is going to jab you in the skin. It should now be obvious what it means.

You don't need to be a scholar to understand Bible prophecy. It's just that until it happens, we're all guessing. You could be the best, the brightest theologian, you're just not going to get it. It's not going to make any sense until it happens. And what does that prove? It proves that nobody doctored the Bible.

Nobody made it up and said, *"Well, I'll try my hand at prophecy. I'm guessing that World War 1 is going to start in Europe, and then World World 2, and immediately after Israel is going to re-birthed, and so I'm going to go write it as if I knew ahead of time, but really, it's all very obvious."* No, none of this is obvious.

You could have been living through the pandemic and yet it

---

1. Maltese, the language of Malta where the Apostle Paul shipwrecked, spells it with a "k": *korona*.

wasn't obvious how it fulfilled the White Horse till you heard my video or read this chapter today. What does that tell us? The God who wrote the Bible is extremely intelligent, foreseeing, all-knowing, trustworthy, and He is trying to get your attention.

You should be paying attention because we're living through the Horses right now. We're not that far off from Jesus' return. He will soon ask us if we have repented of our sins and accepted His sacrifice on the Cross as the ticket to Heaven.

I am so impressed by God's Word. The White Horse is galloping in God's Divine Timeline. The prediction is not made up by man. It can't be. It's not as though somebody knew ahead of time and authored a hoax 2,000 years early:

> "I see the coronavirus happens in the year 2020, so I'm going to pretend to write in riddles, 'A man dressed in white is coming with a corona and he's going to have a sharp toxon that's going to deliver toxic poison.'"

No person made that up. Who did this 2,000 years ago?

God. How much clearer do you need God to speak? Prophecy is the proof of God.

So, who's the person that's riding the White Horse? I got a big clue by what Big Tech censored during the pandemic. As a content creator, I thrive on freedom of speech. During that period of time, we lost our First Amendment rights on social media. They would censor us, suppress our views, hide the like and share functions, and deplatform us for asking questions about the experimental mRNA jabs. There was one person we were not allowed to question:

FAUCI

Anthony Stephen Fauci, born Christmas Eve 1940, became the face of global pandemic response. His middle name *Stephen* is Greek for *corona* in Latin or crown in English. His last name *Fauci* is Italian for "one who makes or uses a sickle," which is the symbol of the Grim Reaper—the Angel of Death.

He often appeared in public dressed in white. He was given a *toxon* and a *corona*, with which he went forth conquering and to conquer.

Before the pandemic, I didn't know who Anthony Stephen Fauci was. He was the highest paid federal bureaucrat in 2022. His salary of $480,654 exceeded the U.S. President's $400,000. He became the longest serving director of the National Institute of Allergy and Infectious Diseases (NIAID[2]), from 1984-2022, overseeing a budget of $6 billion to research HIV/AIDS (the last pandemic). He lied to the public about the origins of the next pandemic he was involved in: COVID-19. He denied that the U.S. funded gain-of-function virus research at the Wuhan Institute of Virology (WIV). Later the National Institute of Health (NIH) admitted to funding the research to the tune of $1.8 million, representing 20% of WIV's coronavirus program.

Fauci was a pretender, a counterfeit savior, who came on the world stage with an mRNA jab (bow) and an engineered virus (corona). Fauci believed or wanted his audience to believe in misinformation about approved drugs (he said Hydroxychloroquine and Ivermectin were "not effective"), natural remedies (he dismissed Vitamins C, D, and Zinc as unproven for viral prevention), and the ineffective masks.

On January 20, 2025, hours before leaving office, Joe Biden gave

---

2. NIAID is one of 27 institutes under the National Institutes of Health (NIH). Fauci's wife, Christine Grady, was Chief of the Department of Bioethics at the NIH Clinical Center from 2012 until April 2025.

Fauci a pre-emptive Presidential Pardon. Fauci's pardon is sweeping in its breadth:

> *Pardon to Dr. Anthony S. Fauci for any and all offenses against the United States which he has committed or may have committed or taken part in during the period from January 20, 1968, through December 31, 2022, including but not limited to any actions, decisions, or omissions in his official capacity as Director of the National Institute of Allergy and Infectious Diseases (NIAID), Chief Medical Advisor to the President, or any other federal role, particularly those related to infectious disease research, public health policy, pandemic response, and testimony before Congress.*

Why would the President pardon someone who committed no crime? The U.S. Supreme Court said in *Burdick v. United States* (1915) that accepting and signing a pardon implies an admission of guilt.

FAUCI = ONE WHO MAKES OR USES A SICKLE.

Fauci dressed in white, had a *toxon* and was given a *corona*. The order is important. Normally the virus comes first, then the vaccine. Revelation 6:2 said the rider had the vaccine (*toxon*) first, then was "given" a coronavirus (*corona* in Latin, *stephanos* in Greek).

It's prophetic that both Fauci and I are named after the Greek noun *stephanos*. His name was written in the passage he fulfills! My name was written in the passage I was assigned to explain to the world in book form and on videos. This message has been burning in my heart and spoken through my lips for 5 years (as I write this in 2025). I had not heard anyone else share this revelation.

> **Revelation 6:2** (NKJV)
>
> 2 And I looked, and behold, a white horse (hippos, ἵππος). He who sat on it had a bow (toxon, τόξον); and a crown (stephanos, στέφανος) was given to him, and he went out conquering (nikōn, νικῶν) and to conquer (nikēsē, νικήσῃ[3]).

---

3. The sports apparel company *Nike* is named after the Greek goddess of Victory. *Nike* means to conquer or have victory.

CHAPTER 9
SORCERY IN THE LAST DAYS

THE LINK to Sorcery

Toxon (translated "bow" in Revelation 6:2) is the poison at the tip of the arrow that they shoot at you. Now we know it refers to pharmaceutical products. From 2020-2023, the global pharmaceutical industry experienced a significant surge in revenue, estimated at over $5.5 trillion. It was the greatest health exploitation of humanity and transfer of wealth in history. Big Pharma paid their executives and shareholders the equivalent of over $1 million every 5 minutes during the pandemic.[1] People became cash cows and test subjects—involuntary human experiments. Do you think God cares?

Out of the 22 judgments of Revelation, the pharmaceutical industry is mentioned in the 1st seal, 6th trumpet, and 7th bowl. Amazingly, the series of judgments starts and ends with a warning about drugs and drug pushers. As far as I know, I am the first Christian to publicly link the White Horse to Anthony Fauci as a

---

1. https://peoplesmedicines.org/resources/media-releases/big-pharma-spent-almost-as-much-enriching-shareholders-as-on-research-and-development-during-pandemic/

person or the WHO as an organization. Fauci stood out during 3.5 years of COVID as "America's top infectious disease expert," leading member of the White House Coronavirus Task Force under President Trump and later Chief Medical Advisor to President Biden.

Up to now, no one else has linked a seal, a trumpet and a bowl to the Pharmaceutical Industry. It's as if God were speaking to us as a parent to a child, "Don't do drugs!"

Though it's not the subject of this book, let's look at one trumpet. At the 6th Shofar judgment (aka 2nd woe), a third of mankind dies. Despite this, they did not give up worshipping demons.

> **Revelation 9:21** [6th Shofar]
> Nor did they repent of their murders [abortion and euthanasia included] or their SORCERIES [*pharmakeiai*] or their sexual immorality [homosexuality] or their thefts [the greatest theft is politicians printing money, over-taxing citizens and re-distributing our wealth to their friends. Legal theft is by far bigger than criminal theft].

The word translated "sorcery" is *pharmekeia* (Greek: φαρμακεία), from which we get the English word "pharmacy." *Pharmakon* (φάρμακον) means drug/poison. *Pharmakeus* (φαρμακεύς) means pharmacist/poisoner/sorcerer. In other words, "sorcery" is dispensing pharmaceutical drugs or poisoning people. To God, sorcery and ingesting or injecting synthetic chemicals are related.

The suggestion is that an experiment far more harmful to health than mRNA jabs will be unleashed, leading to the "excess death" of 1 out of 3 humans. Using today's population of 8 billion, it would mean a genocidal depopulation of 2.67 billion humans just before the Anti-Christ reveals himself. This manufactured health emergency will pave the way for anti-God, totalitarian control.

The 7th and final bowl judgment of God is on Babylon. God judges the Anti-Christ Beast system at the end. The good news is no matter what happens with Anthony Fauci, Bill Gates, lockdowns, and forced vaccines, in the end, all these will be defeated. We are on the winning side. This is the final judgment:

> **Revelation 18:23** (NKJV)
> The light of a lamp shall not shine in you [Babylon] anymore, and the voice of bridegroom and bride shall not be heard in you anymore. For your merchants were the great men of the earth [the billionaires, but in which industry?], for by your SORCERY [*pharmakeia*] all the nations were deceived.

A lot of Christians in America might say, "Not many people still believe in sorcery. How many people follow witches and warlocks anymore? It's in cartoons and movies."

But if you look at the Greek word for "sorcery," you can understand what God is referring to: "*pharmakeia.*" By *pharmakeia* all the nations were deceived. By pharmaceutical drugs or the pharmaceutical propaganda, all the nations were deceived.

We witnessed during the pandemic the level of deception that Big Pharma could bring on the world. Nothing ever came close to its efficacy and speed in causing mass hysteria and psychosis. People who got vaccinated were deathly afraid of walking near someone who was not wearing a mask. I always asked myself, "If the vaccine is effective, and you're vaccinated, why would the unmasked bother you?" No scientific evidence supported the masking of children or healthy adults. Masking became a status symbol of being "in" with the medical "experts" and being a pseudo "hero."

COVID-19 was fatal for 1% of the people who got it. Young people were immune to it. Old people had to have "co-morbidities" (pre-existing conditions) to die from it, but they always listed the cause of death as COVID (not pre-existing conditions). It's so non-scary that most people infected were asymptomatic. That is, they had to get tested to confirm that they had it.

COVID couldn't compare to the bubonic plague, HIV/AIDS or leprosy, where your skin is falling off. Everybody can tell an infected leper when they see one. They cringe and stay away from the sick.

The lab-engineered virus from China wasn't scary enough, so Big Pharma used politicians and mainstream media to coerce people into getting tested and vaccinated. They made it into such a scare, even though many didn't know they had it unless they got tested. They convinced people to get tested and get vaccinated by the billions.

THE DAY OF JUDGMENT

To say God has a special dislike for sorcery/*pharmakeia*/the lies of pharmaceutical companies would not be an exaggeration. I was surprised to see how God describes the coming Day of Judgment.

> **Malachi 3:5**
> "Then I will draw near to you for judgment. I will be a swift witness against the SORCERERS, against the adulterers, against those who swear falsely, against those who oppress the hired worker in his wages, the widow and the fatherless, against those who thrust aside the sojourner, and do not fear me, says the LORD of hosts.

God lists the worst sins He will judge when He holds everybody to account. At the top of His list will be sorcerers, who are the Big Pharma executives, lobbyists, marketers and scientists. He judges them before the adulterers. Why does God single out these people above all the sinners of the world? We are given two clues.

First, God promised to be the Witness in their cases. Do you find that unusual? Christians have always been taught that Jesus will come back as Judge. But in 5 special cases, He personally comes to be a witness. What's in common with all these cases?

They hid their sins and got away with it while they were alive. Big Pharma can hide its data, its studies, its results of harm. Are you allowed to hide your finances? No. Adulterers hide their unfaithfulness. People who oppress others at work hide their sabotaging ways. Adults who abuse elders and orphans don't always have a camera on them; they think they can get away with mistreatment of others. No one saw. But Jesus said, "I saw. In cases where there is no human witness, I will draw near to you for judgment as a witness."

This says a lot about how much was hidden at Wuhan lab and by Anthony Fauci. The collusion between Big Pharma, Big Tech, Mainstream Media, and the politicians who got paid off must have been colossal. Yet those who control the Internet censored us for simply asking questions. Jesus will be the star Witness in these cases.

The second clue why Jesus steps off the bench to become a witness in 5 cases is that "they do not fear me." Imagine the audacity of vaccinating billions of people, isolating children from normal socialization, and controlling people to the point they weren't allowed to talk about natural therapy! These wicked people have "no fear of Me."

As a pastor of 25 years, I can say many sinners have a fear of God. Even Trump said on Air Force One, "I don't think there's anything going to get me in heaven. I really don't. I think I'm not, maybe, heaven-bound. I may be in heaven right now as we fly in Air Force One. I'm not sure I'm gonna be able to make heaven. But

I've made life a lot better for a lot of people."[2]

Some sinners know they need a Savior. They made mistakes but are seeking forgiveness—they're redeemable.

Other sinners are in a class of their own. They lie to children, exploit the innocent, and have the gall to think they should rule the world. No one can be a witness against them because they hold the purse strings, control the judges, and change the rules to suit themselves. They cross every line because to them there is no line. So Jesus will take these cases on personally as the Witness of their attitude and deeds. Isn't Jesus wonderful?

THE LACK OF EVIDENCE

The science of these experimental vaccines remains lacking to this day (2025). Nobody knows the long-term efficacy and the long-term toxic side effects. The sorcery industry pushed a narrative that COVID was a fearful pandemic, that the mRNA jabs were "safe and effective," and that there was no solution other than their expensive products.

We now know that's absolutely false because of India. India's too poor to buy everybody a government-subsidized vaccine. When they experienced a spike, their case load dropped down to normal level within one month by giving out Ivermectin. A cheap, common, anti-parasitic drug for worms, Ivermectin, saved people's lives.

But in Australia and America, it was illegal to take Ivermectin for COVID. Why didn't they tell us that Indians using Ivermectin were not getting as infected? Because Ivermectin costs $1, and the vaccines cost billions of dollars, and Big Pharma got the government to subsidize a mass vaccination program, so it all

---

2. Conversation on Air Force One on October 12, 2025. https://www.the-independent.com/news/world/americas/us-politics/trump-heaven-israel-hamas-gaza-christianity-b2844269.html

translates to a windfall profit for *pharmakeia*. And by *pharmakeia* they deceived the whole world.

CONQUERING THE WORLD

The last clue we're given is that the rider of the White Horse "went out conquering and to conquer." COVID-19 mandates and rules blanketed the Earth. Schools were empty. People worked from home, staring at screens till they became myopic. Neighbors were suspicious of one another; they dobbed on each other (tattled and betrayed one another to police, bosses, and anyone drunk on authority).

During the COVID pandemic, Anthony Fauci's words were like law. Most leaders followed him in lockstep. In country after country, governors, premiers, presidents, doctors, principals, stood up like they were kings of the world, and ordered people to wear masks and keep 6 feet apart. People hung on to their words:

> *"Today. You don't have to wear a mask."*
> *"Oh, today, you DO have to wear a mask."*
> *"You only need ONE shot and we'll flatten the curve."*
> *"No, we need you to have two booster shots to work here or enter our restaurant."*
> *"Lockdown is a temporary measure for your safety."*
> *"We need to extend our emergency powers indefinitely. Lockdowns are here to stay."*

Can you hear what they were doing? They flip-flopped daily because nothing they said was based on long-term, validated data. They were experimenting on us. Unelected health officials relished in controlling people with their ungodly, anti-Christ power.

Is it clear now? Not only does it match perfectly Revelation 6:1-2, it also fulfills another prophecy by Jesus. Let's overlay another Scripture on this.

AS IN THE DAYS OF NOAH

Jesus said, "And as it was in the days of Noah, so it will be also in the days of the Son of Man." (Luke 17:26 NKJV, cf. Matthew 24:37). Now, what's significant about the Days of Noah?

Noah's Flood was the last truly global event in history. Even World War 1 and World War 2 did not include every nation. **COVID-19 was the first worldwide crisis since the days of Noah.** The coronavirus pandemic included every nation; every nation followed the WHO guidelines; every nation went into lockdown. Some came out of it faster.

Sweden avoided harsh lockdowns and relied on voluntary cooperation. They said, "No, we're not going to follow lockdowns. We're going to open our economy. People want to be free." They focused on protecting the elderly. They had no school closures for those under 16. No mask mandates. Sweden did not have more COVID-19 deaths than global averages, and in fact had lower "excess mortality" than Italy and Poland. Most people in the world still don't know this because sorcery is a tool of spiritual seduction, blinding people to the truth, enslaving them to idolatry, and enriching the merchants.

COVID-19 triggered the process of Redemption, just as the first plague of Egypt triggered the process of Exodus out of slavery into the Promised Land. The White Horse has galloped.

But it has left us one more clue—the most important clue to end time prophecy.

> Mimi Mary: You are the voice of reason justice and no sugar coated truth. Pastor Steve!!! Thank you!!

CHAPTER 10
A NEW TIMELINE

THE PANDEMIC WAS SO pivotal to prophecy, the Lord had me predict how they would control us 16 years ago (2009) on my YouTube channel, when I looked a lot younger. Enjoy the transcript:

> *It wouldn't take much for Australia or any country to descend into martial law, and if it's an outbreak of a disease, I've already seen it, I've seen swine flu, SARS, the rumors of it made people go into a lockdown. Imagine a real outbreak where a third of the population dies. You think about that. You have martial law, and if you came out without a mask or you were sick and you had symptoms, martial law generally means "shoot-to-kill" on the spot. Now I know it's very, very frightening and very strange for you to even imagine that, but remember, the Tribulation Scriptures talk about things that are very hard for us to imagine. So, if you want to pray, you need to be praying now for your leaders.*

God is good, isn't He? He told us 11 years before the pandemic came. Amos 3:7 says, "For the Lord God does nothing without revealing his secret to his servants the prophets." Most of what I said has been fulfilled, but not everything. Some of it will continue till the Tribulation—the 7 worst years on earth. My focus is to prepare you ahead of time.

Jesus focused His end-time messages in Matthew 24, Mark 13, and Luke 21 on pre-Tribulation signs. He offered practical advice like where to flee and what kind of weather to avoid, "Pray that your flight may not be in winter..." (Matthew 24:20, Mark 13:18) By reading this book early enough, you should have time to make decisions to help you miss the catastrophes and make it to Heaven.

Another clue Jesus told us:

> **Luke 17:26–27**
> Just as it was in the days of Noah, so will it be in the days of the Son of Man. They were eating and drinking and marrying and being given in marriage, until the day when Noah entered the ark, and the flood came and destroyed them all.

The coronavirus pandemic was the most recent global event since Noah's Flood, so in that way it was like the Days of Noah (Matthew 24:37, Luke 17:26). Now, here's the clincher—the key to unlocking God's timeline. When did it start?

There are a few possible starting points.

- November 17, 2019 was the date of the first confirmed cases in Wuhan, Hubei Province, China.
- The first hospitalization was on December 16, 2019.
- The first public health alert from Wuhan health officials was on December 30, 2019.
- China imposed a lockdown on Wuhan on January 23, 2020.

- If we took an average of those dates, we can say the first outbreak of COVID-19 happened in December 2019.

When did it end? Officially the U.S. public health emergency expired at midnight on May 11, 2023. The following day, May 12, non-U.S. citizens could start traveling into the country without proof of COVID-19 vaccination. I was eyeing this date because we were living in the most locked-down city in the world (Melbourne, Australia), and I was looking for the first opportunity to move my family to the United States, to obey God's call for us over here. God loves America. He has a lot of mercy on Americans.

Since the Lord had spoken to me to leave Australia, and go to the America, dates when travel restrictions lifted were important to me.

- China dropped the pre-departure COVID-19 testing requirement on April 29, 2023.
- Japan fully normalized air travel on May 8, 2023.
- The U.S. allowed foreigners to enter without proof of vaccination on May 12, 2023.
- Brazil stopped requiring vaccine proof and tests for entry in May 2023.

How long did the pandemic last? It started in December 2019 and ended in May 2023. Count that! God made it so easy to see. How many years?

Three and a half. Where have we seen that before? The Bible prophecy teacher in me said, "We've got patterns that have been marked out in the Book of Daniel, in the Book of Revelation, and in all the Gospels."

- Jesus ministered 3.5 years.
- The Two Witnesses will minister 3.5 years.

- Daniel and Revelation both predict the Anti-Christ will oppress the saints for 3.5 years.

There are periods of 3.5 years over and over in the Bible. Here's a complete list of 9 references. Plus scholarly estimates of the duration of Jesus' earthly ministry [counting feast days mentioned in the Gospels] come to 3.5 years, making a total of 10 references. Ten is a strong confirmation. God wants us to pay attention to this cycle!

TIME, TIMES, AND HALF A TIME

Daniel 7:25

He [Anti-Christ] shall speak words against the Most High, and shall wear out the saints of the Most High, and shall think to change the times and the law; and they shall be given into his hand for a time, times, and half a time [= 3.5 years].

Daniel 12:7

And I heard the man clothed in linen, who was above the waters of the stream; he raised his right hand and his left hand toward heaven and swore by him who lives forever that it would be for a time, times, and half a time [= 3.5 years], and that when the shattering of the power of the holy people comes to an end all these things would be finished.

Revelation 12:14

But the woman [Israel] was given the two wings of the great eagle so that she might fly from the serpent into the wilderness, to the place where she is to be nourished for a time, and times, and half a time [= 3.5 years].

42 MONTHS

> **Revelation 11:2**
> but do not measure the court outside the temple; leave that out, for it is given over to the [Gentile] nations, and they will trample the holy city for forty-two months [= 3.5 years].
>
> **Revelation 13:5**
> And the beast was given a mouth uttering haughty and blasphemous words, and it was allowed to exercise authority for forty-two months [= 3.5 years].

1,260 DAYS

> **Revelation 11:3**
> And I will grant authority to my two witnesses, and they will prophesy for 1,260 days [= 3.5 years], clothed in sackcloth.
>
> **Revelation 12:6**
> and the woman [Israel] fled into the wilderness [Jordan or Saudi Arabia], where she has a place prepared by God, in which she is to be nourished for 1,260 days [= 3.5 years].

Three and a half years is a time marker. The pattern of 3.5 years had just been fulfilled by COVID-19. Whoever said that 3.5 years was only going to happen once?

Bible teachers assumed that. They see the Anti-Christ's power will last 3.5 years. They also see correctly the bowls of wrath will last 3.5 years. Then they wrongly assumed that the seals and trumpets will last 3.5 years.

We saw in Chapter 7, many reasons why cramming the seals and trumpets into 3.5 years doesn't make sense. The trumpets should theoretically last 3.5 years, but nothing in the text says so. You see, we have a lot of assumptions.

The Bible infers that the duration of the 7 Trumpets (Shofars) is equal to the duration of the 7 Bowls. Together they would add up to 7 years. That matches with Daniel's 70th Week (a week of years is 7 years). The only explicit duration we have for any trumpet is the fifth trumpet (or the first woe). It's repeated twice:

> **Revelation 9:5**
> They were allowed to torment them for FIVE MONTHS, but not to kill them, and their torment was like the torment of a scorpion when it stings someone.
>
> **Revelation 9:10** They have tails and stings like scorpions, and their power to hurt people for FIVE MONTHS is in their tails.

We shouldn't assume every trumpet lasts the same amount of time, but let's use the law of averages. If the 5th trumpet equals 5 months, and there are 7 trumpets, then on average we estimate the 7 trumpets will last 35 months (one month shy of 3 years). That's close to 3.5 years.

The only prophet foretold by name to return in the End Times is Elijah.[1] Is it a surprise, 3.5 years are mentioned in connection with him—both times in the New Testament?

3.5 YEARS

Luke 4:25

---

1. The doctrine of Elijah's return is well established in Malachi 3:1, 4:5-6, Matthew 11:13-14, 17:10-13, Luke 1:17, and Revelation 11:3-6. Jews are so expectant of Eliyahu's coming to herald the arrival of Messiah that they reserve an empty chair for him during each Passover Seder and pour a fifth cup of wine for him, left untouched at the table. During a boy's circumcision (brit milah), an empty chair is also reserved for Eliyahu who's expected to come resolve halachic (legal) disputes.

> But in truth, I tell you, there were many widows in Israel in the days of Elijah, when the heavens were shut up three years and six months [= 3.5 years], and a great famine came over all the land.
>
> **James 5:17**
>
> Elijah was a man with a nature like ours, and he prayed fervently that it might not rain, and for three years and six months [= 3.5 years] it did not rain on the earth.

This pattern matches perfectly with the careers of the Two Witnesses lasting 1,260 days (Rev 11:3). Elijah is one of the Two Witnesses who will come back to earth to minister to the Jews.

What if three and a half years is a time marker that we're not supposed to assume will occur only once? It didn't just happen with Jesus once, it's going to happen with the Anti-Christ, it's going to happen during the first half of the Tribulation, and it's going to happen again during the second half (the Great Tribulation). Is it possible that it happens during the pre-Tribulation signs?

If we allow God's Word to speak to us, and we have no assumption or theology to defend, then we can let the Bible show us where it's taking us.

The White Horse Took 3.5 Years

Having lived through the COVID-19 pandemic, we can now conclusively agree the First Seal, the White Horse, took three and a half years. Can we then project? Is it possible the other horses will also last three and a half years?

I began to tell my Church, as soon as June comes, we're going to have the Red Horse and the Red Horse means, among many things, war. A war likely sparked by Islam.

CHAPTER 11
THE RED HORSE

2ND SEAL: **The Red Horse**

 REVELATION 6:3-4 (NKJV)
3 When He opened the second seal, I heard the second living creature saying, "Come and see."
4 Another horse, fiery red, went out. And it was granted to the one who sat on it to take peace from the earth, and that people should kill one another; and there was given to him a great sword.

There's so much meaning to this. What can red symbolize?

Red = Blood, Fire, War, Communism, or Marxism. They're all symbolized by the color red.

"Take Peace from the Earth." If you read this in Hebrew, it's very clear what it means. The word "Earth" in Hebrew is *"Eretz."* Eretz is synonymous with "the nation or the Land of Israel." When you say the *Eretz*, it can mean the "whole earth," but it can specifically mean Israel. So, this verse was predicting that when the Red Horse comes, he will take peace from Israel. In other words, the October 7, 2023 Attack would happen.

Great Sword = the Sword of Islam, Direct Energy Weapons (DEWs), Electro-Magnetic Pulse Bombs (EMPs), Nuclear Weapons, or John the Revelator could be referring to an unknown weapon that has not yet been released.

A "great sword" means a "great weapon" or a "mega weapon," something John could not describe 2,000 years ago. He certainly could not fathom Islam coming to deny everything he preached and wrote about as an eye witness. A **"mega sword"** may be a literal sword, but it could be something beyond. Who's going to be afraid of a huge sword? If an attacker carried a 7-foot sword, that wouldn't necessarily make him more fearsome. It'd be very hard to drag that sword around. So, the word "mega sword" suggests a weapon that John couldn't describe any better, so he said, *"Watch out for a mega weapon!"* What can that be? We now have nuclear weapons, EMPs, and DEWs.

But if you prefer to take it literally, you do have one group of people in the world that is symbolized by a great sword: it's on their flag, the flag of Islam. The flag of Saudi Arabia is green with a white sword. So, at every level, God's Word is true and giving us clues. The Red Horse took peace away from *Eretz Israel* by a "great sword" during the time of the Red Horse.

Another prophecy about who would attack Israel, is hidden in the beginning of the Bible:

> **Genesis 6:11**
> Now the earth was corrupt in God's sight, and the earth was filled with violence.

Even though the text applies at first glance to the days of Noah, there is a double entendre applying further to our times. In Hebrew, this verse reads: "and the *Eretz* was filled with *Hamas*." Yes, that's right, God knew from the beginning that the main enemy of Israel would be named *Hamas*—a name which reveals their nature in

Hebrew, "violence." Hamas carried out the worst attack on Israel since its birth.

October 7 was truly grotesque because it was not only the slaughter of civilians by Islamic terrorists, but they paraded these victims (concert goers) in the streets, their fellow Palestinians participated in celebrating the carnage, some Jewish women were raped and had their breasts cut off, some parents watched their child killed in front of them inside their homes, and some concert goers were stopped and burned alive in their cars. All in the name of Hamas.

8 YEARS OF PROPHETIC WARNING

On October 6, I had an urgency in my spirit to put up a YouTube video and tell the world, "War is imminent."[1] The next day, October 7, it happened. Anything that doesn't happen immediately results in critics calling me a false prophet. Anything that does happen immediately—they're all silent, waiting for my next prediction to nitpick. I found out it's not hard to please God; it's hard to please some Christians! In this case, the prophecy did happen immediately... it was tragic, but God warned us about it.

Israel at War Confirms the Red Horse of Revelation 6 | Adjust Your Timeline Oct 11, 2023 YouTube censored this video and removed the share button. See it for yourself: https://www.youtube.com/watch?v=ozpz2yuEhhc

Eight years before October 7, I posted a warning that Israel would be attacked, the IDF taken by surprise, and Jewish hostages taken. It got nearly 2 million views. It was titled "15 Year Old Secular Jewish Boy Nathan's Vision of WWIII on Blood Moon: Gog Magog Future of Israel." Some things have unfolded exactly as

---

1. YouTube censors this video so that it's not searchable by exact title or with my name added. Watch it for yourself: https://www.youtube.com/watch?v=L9LMR8vAgKo

predicted, while others wait to be fulfilled. Thank God, He warns Jews and Christians.

I don't take credit because it wasn't directly my prediction, but I was paying attention to what God was showing in dreams and visions. It's part of my job. Sometimes I get a dream or revelation, other times somebody else gets a dream or vision and I want to evaluate it according to the standard of the Bible.

A young Jewish boy named Nathan (Natan in Hebrew) was given a vision of the End Time, and though he had not read the New Testament and purportedly did not believe in our Messiah (though He's their Messiah as well), his vision was in line with Biblical Revelation.

Eight years ago, I said in this video, "This vision lines up with the Bible. Do with it what you'd like." It took a few years to be fulfilled. People who accused me of being a "false prophet" for promoting a Jewish boy were proven false.

After the October 7 Attack, I made an anniversary video of Natan's Vision so you can see it on YouTube, reminding people that what he said partially has been fulfilled, and therefore, we may expect the rest of it to be fulfilled. Let's go over the unfulfilled part:

> The boy's rabbi asked him, *"Do you know who Gog is, the one that's going to come and attack Israel?"*
> Natan said, *"Don't you know?"*
> The rabbi said, *"No, I don't know. Who is Gog? Who did you see?"* (Gog is the arch-enemy of Israel that will attack Israel in the last days, and guess what? It is not Russia or Putin.)
> The young man said, *"Don't you know? It's Obama. Obama is going to come back."*

My spirit is perturbed by Obama. I believe he has a hidden agenda and he'll be back. When I said this at that time, some called me a false prophet on social media. They said, "Well, there you go!

You're a false prophet for sure because Obama has finished his second term and he cannot come back (to the White House)."

Interestingly, Obama bought a home in Washington, D.C. and never left during the Trump years. He actively campaigned for Joe Biden in what many conservatives still call the *Stolen Election* of 2020. Obama flew to meet the Prime Minister of the UK and the King of Belgium as recently as March 18, 2024 and March 17, 2025 respectively. That privilege should be reserved only for the President of the United States or his delegate. Why is Obama representing the United States at such events? So, far from being false, it's just taking a few years for it to be fulfilled.

Now, I don't yet know for sure that Gog is the same as the Anti-Christ. Gog may be the Anti-Christ or Gog may be another character within this end time arena of many bad guys whom the Bible talks about. Natan did not see Russia as Gog, but given enough push, Russia may be the one to take America out because of her own cup of sins.

IRAN

At the same time Israel was dealing with Hamas and the hostages, Israel fought a war against Iran. For decades, Iran had been waging a proxy war against Israel by funding and enabling Hamas in Gaza, Hezbollah in Lebanon, and Houthis in Yemen. Iran was also concealing enriched uranium and developing nuclear weapons. Fearing the worst and not getting help from the international community, Israel did the world a favor by making a preemptive strike on Iran's nuclear sites on June 13, 2025.

Iran retaliated by sending 525 ballistic missiles and 300 drones into Israel. President Trump stepped in by dropping 14 bunker busting bombs on Iran's *Fordow, Natanz, and Isfahan*, on June 22, 2025. The Iran military leadership was nearly eliminated. The political leadership that remained was shaken by American military might. By June 24, the Twelve Day War ended.

The proof that our prophetic model is inspired lies in its ability to predict. By it, I confidently opposed most American prophecy preachers' predictions and accurately foretold:

1. Iran would fight against Israel.
2. Russia would not join the fight. Putin said he would not support Iran and advised Iranian leadership to agree quickly with Trump.
3. Israel would win but there would be no lasting peace. Hamas will attack again. Iran will attack again.
4. One day, further down the line, Iran will successfully build its nuclear weapons and use them. But not now.

As the Lord showed me, there was no Ezekiel 38 War. Russia was not Gog. Iran did not win. President Trump believes that he brokered lasting peace between Israel and Hamas. I do not believe this is possible during the Red Horse of War.

THE NEXT WAR | RUSSIA, RUSSIA, RUSSIA

Russia does not want to have war with the United States or Europe, but it may be provoked into having one in 2026. One of the most audacious "false flags" was the West sabotaging the Nordstream 1 & 2 pipelines. On September 26, 2022, a series of underwater explosions damaged three of the four pipelines in the Baltic Sea. No one but an advanced Western government has the technology or capability to blow up pipes sitting at great depth beneath the ocean, while being undetected. Till now (2025) no international investigation has confirmed a perpetrator and no charges have been filed. Western powers alleged that Russia blew up its own pipeline. Russia is enriched by Europe's reliance on its oil and gas. What incentive would it have to cut itself off at the knees? The likely perpetrator was Ukraine.[2]

Despite such an obviously staged provocation, and attempt at *gaslighting on a global scale*, Russia remained composed. Putin did not react or retaliate militarily. But you can push a person too far, and I believe this is Europe/ NATO's intention in 2026, before the US election. A World War 3 in 2026. This would throw Europe's economy into chaos, which is one scenario to set us up for the Black Horse.

There was another provocation in March 22, 2024: a major terrorist attack on Crocus City Hall near Moscow, just before a concert was scheduled to start. People were there to enjoy music when 4 men hiding their faces entered. They murdered about 145 concert attendees. The Kremlin said on the same day that Russia was now in a state of war.

Who were these men? They ran straight to the Ukrainian border. One captured and interrogated by the Russians confessed he was contacted and offered money on Telegram. Ukraine is currently the proxy for the West to fight Russia. America has not declared war. We just send over money and arms, so technically America is not at war with Russia, but America is active. NATO is active. Europe is active.

Be careful about the US/European/Western narrative. Right away, we were told that ISIS claimed responsibility for the attack. It is possible they claim responsibility for things that they have nothing to do with, just because it agrees with their goals. I have a few questions:

- *How did we know so quickly?* Remember 9/11, when President Bush took several months to confirm the identity and motives of the perpetrators. In the case of Russia, we blamed ISIS the next day and the US media ran with that narrative. It was so fast.

---

2. https://www.bbc.com/news/articles/cnvyz1472rpo

- *Why did these four attackers hide their faces?* In the past, ISIS and al-Qaeda members on a suicide mission wanted to be known. They don't mind showing their faces. Typically Muslim terrorists record and publish a pre-attack video to glorify *Allah*, but we don't have any of that.
- Why also did none of the attackers shout, *"Allahu Akbar"?* Isn't that what Muslims always shout? Few people know what this means. The media always mistranslates it as "God is great." No, that would be *"Allahu Kabir."*[3] *"Allah Akbar"* (called the *takbir*) means "Allah is greater," which is of course an incomplete sentence. Greater than what? Islam came after Judaism and Christianity, so the implied meaning is "Allah is greater than *Elohim/Yahweh* the Jewish God," "Allah is greater than *Jesus* the Son of God," and "Allah is greater than the American God of the Bible." Some Muslims may deny this and say, "We worship the same God." Ask them one question to determine how sincere they are, "If we worship the same God, why aren't Christians and Jews allowed to pray on the Temple Mount? Why only Muslims can pray to Allah and Jews and Christians are to keep silent?" I lead tours to Israel and it's literally illegal for tourists to pray there. Islamists don't believe they worship the same God as we do. They want to declare that Islam is greater than your religion and Allah is greater than your God, but historically Islamic countries lose to Christian countries, and it loses to Israel, so the constant defeats create a theological contradiction. Islamists will keep shouting *"Allahu*

---

3. There are 3 forms to an adjective: positive, comparative and superlative.
   Positive: *Allahu Kabir* (great)
   Comparative: *Allahu Akbar* (greater)
   Superlative: *Allahu al-Akbar* (the greatest)

Akbar" before every terror attack. Not once did the 4 attackers use the word "Allah" or the *takbir* during the attack on Russians, nor did the criminal caught use the word during his interrogation.
- Why did the attackers leave the concert a couple of minutes before Russian special forces arrived? Why did they run and hide? That is not Islamic martyrdom.
- Why did they flee to Ukraine? Three out of four were caught fleeing at Ukraine border. None of them looked like an Arab or had a beard. Putin claimed that handlers promised them a "window" or safe passage to Belarus. One of them died during the Russian style "interrogation." They found out that each of these men were promised only US$5,000. Imagine taking a hundred lives for merely $5,000! They said they were contacted anonymously through Telegram and they were not fully paid. That was their complaint after they got arrested.

Conspiracy theorist Alex Jones claimed it was a NATO/CIA "cut out" destabilizing Russia. Whether you believe him or not, Jones has been accurate on globalist plans and cover up stories.

In case you're not familiar with the term "cut out", let me explain what a CIA cut out is. When the CIA wants to do something, but they don't want to have responsibility, they form or hire another group to do exactly what they want to do, and let them take responsibility. That's a cut-out.

Consider what Alex Jones is alleging: that there is a CIA cut out operating in Europe. To do what? **To provoke World War 3.**

Dmitry Medvedev, the Chairman of the Security Council of the Russian Federation said on 23 March 2024:

> "If it is established that these are terrorists of the Kyiv regime, it is impossible to deal with them and their ideological inspirers differently. All of them

must be found and mercilessly destroyed as terrorists. Including officials of the state that committed such atrocity. Death for death."[4]

Russia is not like America, where we show mercy and compassion on illegals and criminals. Around the time of this attack on Russia, the Obama-appointed US District Judge Sharon Johnson Coleman ruled that illegals can buy and own guns. Isn't that amazing? In America, we try to take away guns from citizens and give them to illegals.

Russia is not like us. Russia says, "No mercy on people who kill our civilians while watching a concert." They got information out of torturing these men. This information did not lead to ISIS. This may lead to NATO. By the way, NATO is us. We are not always the good guys.

Another curious fact is John Kirby, the White House National Security Communications Advisor under Biden, issuing a warning two weeks before the Russian theater attack. He "put out a notice to **all Americans in Moscow** to avoid any large gathering, **concerts**, obviously, shopping malls, anything like that."[5]

How did John Kirby know that an attack would happen on Russian soil at a concert two weeks before it happened? It suggested that Alex Jones might be right about the shadow government: the CIA controls the Elites, the Media, the Narrative, and the World.

They provoked Russia by bombing the Nordstream Pipeline—it didn't work. They provoked again by attacking Russian civilians on

---

4. Russia Today, 23 March 2024: https://www.rt.com/russia/594740-medvedev-terrorists-death-response/
5. Even though this was widely corroborated, the official website of the U.S. Embassy in Russia has removed the notice. C-SPAN still has the video of John Kirby: https://www.c-span.org/clip/public-affairs-event/john-kirby-calls-images-from-moscow-concert-hall-attack-horrible/5111305. Newsweek reported on March 22, 2024 the advance warning to avoid concerts: https://www.newsweek.com/us-embassy-warned-americans-avoid-moscow-concerts-weeks-before-attacks-1882548

Russian soil—it didn't work. They will continue until Russia retaliates. Then the narrative will be, "**Russia started it.**"

Russian civilians must wonder how they get blamed. They were the ones who got attacked during a concert right in the heart of their capital city."

FRANCE IS STRATEGIC

Let's go back to when the Red Horse started galloping. I prophesied that it would have to start in June 2023.

One June 27, 2023, the whole nation of France erupted in riots when one 17-year-old Muslim driver named Nahel Merzouk[6] was shot dead by French police. 45,000 police, gendarmes and counter-terrorism forces were called out on the streets to quell the riots. Turmoil spilled over to Belgium. All for one underage Muslim driver who was stopped at a traffic light, then he ran away from the police.

Under a 2017 law, designed to prevent "vehicular terrorism," French police are authorized to use deadly force if they believe a car driver is driving recklessly and may kill people. To the rest of the world, vehicular terrorism was a new thing. It happened once in Melbourne, Australia on December 21, 2017. Saeed Noori was an Afghan who arrived in Australia in 2004. Inspired by ISIS, he rammed his car into pedestrians on Flinders Street, then got out to stab people, injuring a total of 19 people. In France, Germany, England, and Spain, car ramming is more frequent. Since the lunar tetrad of 2014 and 2015, we watched on the news a lot of people mowed over by trucks and cars, especially on national or Christian holidays. On July 14, 2016, a Tunisian man named Mohamed Lahouaiej Bouhlel drove a truck into a crowd in Nice celebrating Bastille Day, killing 86 people and injuring 434 people.[7]

---

6. A French national of Algerian-Moroccan descent.
7. Le Hars, Anne (1 December 2017). "*Attentat de Nice : six mois après, trois*

So they made a new law to prevent it.

This young man was an underaged truck driver, he's got a rap sheet that shows he's been in trouble with the law before, and he's violating this anti-vehicular terrorism law. I don't know how badly he was driving, how many pedestrians were in his way, or if he deserved to be killed, but he shouldn't have run away from police.

The French police are on edge because there are now suburbs in Paris that are no go zones. The Muslim residents live under a separate law/Sharia. That's coming to the rest of the Western world.

At that time, there were many acts of terror, all coming from one particular group of people. So for whatever reason, the police thought that they had to open fire and they killed this 17-year-old, whom Western media dishonestly describes as a delivery truck driver. What a farcical description of a 17-year-old, Muslim criminal.

That's really the proper description. If you understand the story objectively, you can hide the identity of the victim or perpetrator. Who's a truck driver? It could be almost any one of us. No, this was a Muslim criminal named Nahel Merzouk. If you want the community to be safe, identify criminals.

This is important for the next part of the story. Truck drivers were not up in arms about the truck driver's death. Muslims nationwide went on a violent rampage. They identified him as a fellow Muslim. Was their violence and looting the way to seek justice? You can see videos where they go into shops and start stealing Volkswagens. What's the logic? There's no justice for this truck driver until Muslims get to drive free Volkswagens?

You can also see the looting of luxury retail shops and the burning down of churches. So there's no justice until Christians are punished, was that it? Christian churches were completely unrelated to the story, but to the Muslim residents, it was an

---

personnes toujours hospitalisées". France 3 Provence-Alpes-Côte d'Azur (in French). Retrieved 2025-10-20.

opportunity to assert dominance. One "young French man" (unnamed) offered bounties on Twitter (now X) on June 28–29, 2023 for harming police: €550 for one hand cut off, €1,200 for both hands, and €2,000 for the officer's death. The man remained *unnamed* all the way to his sentencing on July 10, 2023, when he received 1 year in prison.

What we saw in France was the galloping of the Red Horse. I could predict this to the month because of the revelation that the White Horse was none other than Fauci, a man who wears a white coat, had a bow and arrow (*toxon*) and was given a crown (*corona*), with which he went conquering the world with ineffective policies that enslaved people and enriched Big Pharma.

For people who were not content creators like I am, they may have not realized YouTube and Big Tech's endeavor to hide all this. Content creators lived through three and a half years of lies and censorship. If we so much as asked questions about Fauci or the vaccines, we were given strikes. Some were summarily deplatformed, which meant they lost their influence and livelihood without warning.

What's interesting now is that we have been given a very specific timeline. We know exactly how long the White horse galloped for. We know when all of this started. I'll say January 2020, but if you want to be technical, it began towards the end of December 2019. That's when we started hearing rumors of COVID-19, but the full on scare campaign began in January 2020. That's when we knew something was amiss.

Suddenly there was a big pharmaceutical push for the whole world to believe a certain story. In the beginning, we saw videos out of China that this virus was meant to send its victims into convulsion and spasms. Chinese people were falling all over the place, on the streets of Wuhan, like they had epilepsy.

For some reason, we never saw it happen anywhere else. But that was the story in January 2020. That was being played in front of us. Then the media personalities and politicians, most of whom couldn't explain 11th grade science, said you're irresponsible if you didn't take the jab. You were going to kill the vaccinated. The claim that the unvaccinated were putting everybody else in danger is now proven false in Australia, because the *statistics of people who died after they got vaccinated was counted among the unvaccinated.*

Can you believe that? If you were vaccinated and died within three weeks, you were called *unvaccinated*. So there's how you can twist statistics. We found out all this because rebel politicians would release the data on Twitter (now X) after Elon Musk bought it for $44 billion. Twitter/X is a reclaimed platform where we can speak freely, for now.

This is what we've all lived through. We look back and see that it transpired in the space of 3.5 years. As of June 2023, no country requires you to wear a mask, social distance or be vaccinated.

It's ineffective. The virus is still around, the flu is still around, but none of that seems to matter now. What matters is that we now know how long it lasted. Three and a half years. The moment it stopped, the next Horseman rode in June 27, 2023. On the dot. On the nose. We are living in the Red Horse as I write this.

FULFILLMENTS & PREDICTIONS

Red is a common symbol for blood, fire, war, and Marxism/communism/socialism. During the period of the Red Horse, we see all these unusual and intense activities:

- **June 27—July 5, 2023:** The Red Horse started with the Muslim riots in France.
- **August 8–10, 2023:** Maui Wildfires. The deadliest U.S. wildfire in a century. Wind-driven fires devastated Lahaina and parts of Maui. Strange aspects included the rapid spread on a non-wildfire-prone island, failure to warn the public (even though such systems are tested regularly on Hawaii), suspicion of land grab motives,

theories of near-infrared direct energy weapon (DEW), pictures of blue roofs spared (near-infrared range would be invisible to the naked eye but have a minimal reaction with objects colored blue). 102 died, 2,200 homes and structures were destroyed, totaling $5.5 billion of damages.

- **October 7, 2023:** Hamas Attack on the Supernova Sukkot concert attendees. Hamas killed 1,200 people and took 251 people from over 20 countries as hostages. The 20 last survivors were released on October 13, 2025, after being held in captivity for 738 days.
- **February–March 2024:** Texas Panhandle Wildfires, the largest in Texas history, burning 1.1 million acres. Strange aspects: Ignited during cold snap (unusual for winter), rapid growth despite weather, theories of arson or energy policy links. Impacts: 2 deaths, thousands of cattle lost, 500+ structures burned; affected 15 counties.
- **February 4, 2024:** The U.S. and U.K. launched strikes against Houthi targets in Yemen to protect Red Sea shipping.
- **January 7-31, 2025:** Los Angeles Fires. 14 wildfires burned for 24 days during the winter (an unusual off-season condition), killing 440 people and destroying 18,000 homes. Over 200,000 people evacuated. Water shortages during the fires were highly unusual and contributed significantly to the severity of the fires. President Trump blamed Gavin Newsom's poor water management and state environmental policies, such as diverting water away to the ocean in the name of protecting a small endangered fish few had heard of prior to the fire—the delta smelt. On January 27, 2025, Trump signed an executive order directing federal agencies to override California's water allocation rules

and billions of gallons were released from two Central Valley dams in early February 2025.

- **February 28, 2025:** Zelensky dishonored Trump. I warned that Zelenskyy was an actor and Trump would not get the peace deal he was expecting. If my timeline of the Red Horse is correct, there will be no peace in Ukraine. On a highly publicized scheduled visit to the Oval Office, Ukrainian President Volodymyr Zelenskyy was supposed to sign a historic mineral revenue-sharing deal with President Trump. Instead, on cue like the actor that he is, he performed a drama in front of the press, disrespected President Donald Trump and even threatened him: "During the war, everybody has problems, even you, but you have a nice ocean and don't feel it now, but you will feel it in the future." Trump replied, ""You're gambling with World War 3." Trump also called Zelenskyy "ungrateful." Immediately after this attempt to one-up Trump in his own White House, Zelenskyy flew to meet European leaders who immediately applauded him. It looked staged and coordinated from my limited perspective. Trump was played and the Europeans were gleeful. Despite the U.S. President's sincere hopes of peace in Ukraine, the Bible gave us better intel than he had. (Updated on Oct 31, 2025: Trump's planned Budapest summit with Putin got canceled. As predicted, the Red Horse signals war.)
- **October 13, 2025:** As part of Trump's terms for a ceasefire/peace in the Middle East, Hamas released all 20 living hostages in exchange for nearly 2000 Palestinian prisoners. I don't know whether or not Hamas realizes how humiliating it is that the life of 1 Jewish person equals that of 100 Palestinians. As I predicted, Hamas violated the ceasefire and refused to release the bodies of 28 deceased Israeli as part of the handover. President

Trump's mistake was to act like King Saul and spare the enemies. War will never end with Hamas. Even Saudi Arabia threatened to walk away from any further negotiations with Israel as long as Hamas was allowed to remain in power. The Arabs know who the terrorists are.

Till the end of 2026, the Red Horse will continue to gallop. There will be surprising wars erupting in unexpected places. One of those seems to be Venezuela. From September 2, 2025 to November 15, 2025, Trump authorized military airstrikes against 22 "narco boats," killing 83 drug traffickers. By November 16, a military build up of 12,000 U.S. troops on 12 ships in the Caribbean pointed to a possible invasion of Venezuela to overthrow communist leader Nicolás Maduro.

This would bring justice to many Venezuelans oppressed by communism. It would also give the USA access to the world's largest reserve of oil, driving oil price down. A flood of cheap oil on the world market would accomplish at least three objectives in the Trump doctrine: 1) lower the prices of goods for Americans, 2) create America's energy independence by not relying on its top foreign sources (Canada, Mexico and Saudi Arabia), and 3) weaken the Russian economy, which relies on energy exports for 30-40% of its federal budget revenues. You can expect more wars.

> Mindy Davis: I am so thankful that you made this video [Global Financial Crash 2024 | Will IRAN Start WW3] Brother Steve. I have been praying to the Lord concerning [other Youtube channels'] prophetic videos that are telling of events to come. It has been very frightening and confusing, because they fall under future judgements that seem quite out of sequence from I am reading in the Bible. You have helped me to calm down and feel peace again. God bless you!

CHAPTER 12
THE ECLIPSES &
THE SIGN OF JONAH

AMERICA'S LAST WARNING

A WORLD without America would be a radically different place. America has 235 million Christians and 375,000 churches, more than any other country. America, for better and for worse, is the world's Big Brother. America polices global conflicts. Both Israel and Iran must call up President Trump to ask for permission to bomb each other.[1] President Trump says, "Yes, but don't go too far." America is like an umpire at her best, and a vampire at her worst.

Many Bible prophecy teachers have speculated why America,

---

1. Before "Operation Rising Lion" against Iran on June 13, 2025, Israel informed U.S. officials, including Secretary of State Marco Rubio. https://www.bbc.com/news/articles/cm2kd2k3mv7o

Trump said he was "fully in the loop" and even knew of "the next already planned attacks." https://www.theguardian.com/us-news/2025/jun/13/trump-iran-israel-attacks-response

Before Iran launched missile attacks on the U.S. Al Udeid Air Base in Qatar on June 23, 2025, Iran provided Trump with "early notice" to allow U.S. personnel to evacuate and minimizing casualties. Trump allowed Iran to save face and project confidence, a part of "de-escalation diplomacy." https://www.cbsnews.com/news/trump-iran-early-notice-qatar-attacks-us-base/

being the supremely important nation on world stage (it owns the world's reserve currency, has the world's largest economy, the world's mightiest military) is not mentioned in the Bible. I believe it is mentioned, but there's not a great mention.

When I overlay the warning of the 3 Great American solar eclipses (2017-2024) with the Red Horse (2023.5-2027), there is an overlap. This suggests in the zone of a surprise attack on American soil that will end its dominance.

When you look in American history, each time we had a series of solar eclipses, it coincided with war. (One standalone eclipse coincided with pestilence.) Now, we have a conjunction of signs saying, regrettably, peace and prosperity won't last. Something bad is going to happen with the United States that will be war-like. The assassination of Charlie Kirk on September 10, 2025, seems only the beginning of attacks on Christians.

10 SOLAR ECLIPSES

Whereas blood moons (lunar eclipses) tend to be signs for Israel, darkened suns (solar eclipses) tend to be omens for the nations—the Gentiles. The greatest Gentile nation on the planet is the United States of America. Here's a brief look at the history of eclipses coinciding with war or disaster in the United States.

- In **1778** and **1780**, there were solar eclipses going across the United States. Both came in the middle of the **American Revolutionary War** (1775-1783, 8 years and 4 months).
- In **1860** and **1869**, there were solar eclipses going across the United States. One was in the middle of the **American Civil War** (1861-1865); the other during the aftermath of America's deadliest war (2-3 times worse than WW2). Having lost 750,000 Americans, the nation was trying to rebuild.

- The **1918 eclipse** coincided with the **Spanish flu** outbreak, which killed more people than died in World War 1.
- In **1970** and **1979** there were solar eclipses going across the United States. Nobody paid attention in those days. The churches never talked about this back then. Now we look back and we can see, those were omens in the middle of the **Vietnam War** (1965-1973), a conflict that completely reshaped this nation.
- From **2017** to **2024**, America experienced 3 solar eclipses. That makes 10 eclipses in total crossing the continental United States since its birth. If the prophetic pattern hold up, and if we are in the Red Horse, then everything points to one thing—WAR. Could it be America's 2nd Civil War? Could it be a catastrophic war with Russia? Or will it be a continuation of the War with Islam that started on September 11, 2001?

PSYCHOLOGICAL CONDITIONING FOR CIVIL WAR

A movie came out at exactly the same time as the eclipse in April 8, 2024. It was called *"Civil War."* Are the Hollywood elites conditioning us to accept this?

Before the COVID pandemic, did you realize that Hollywood put out a lot of movies about epidemics? And then the pandemic came!

Are they using movies to sow division and pre-program Americans to hate each other? The movie features an intense scene where a journalist pleads for U.S. soldiers not to shoot them, "Just, please...We're American, ok?" The soldier responded, "OK. What kind of American are you?"

We now have Americans who distinguish themselves as "Trump-supporting American" versus "Illegal-Immigrant-supporting American," "Climate-Change-supporting American," or

"UN-supporting American." It grieves me to see this. It grieves me to hear the amount of division. We are one people, "one Nation under God, indivisible, with liberty and justice for all."[2]

Since patterns are prophetic, a civil war is entirely possible again. America is her own worst enemy.

TRUMP'S ROLE IN THE END

Anyone who's read my books, *President Trump's Pro-Christian Accomplishments* and *Trump's Unfinished Business,* knows that I am not pro-Trump as much as I am pro-Christian, pro-church, pro-Israel, pro-life, pro-freedom, and therefore, I am pro-Trump.

How then can Trump be the President who will see the decline or the end of America? It doesn't make sense to the natural mind.

As I watch Trump negotiate the end of seven wars, the release of hostages, and fairer trade deals, I see a genius and celebrate his victories. No one else could have done it so well. I see Biblical justice being manifested in this mighty nation. I rejoice at the return of the Bible and prayer in public schools.

Pete Hegseth, Secretary of War, has reformed the military, dismantling "woke" culture, banning transgenders from service, ending the emphasis on sensitivity and diversity, and returning to "old school" rigorous training. The FBI is investigating the bad guys —James Comey former FBI Director (for obstruction of justice and lying under oath) and John Bolton former national security adviser (mishandling sensitive documents). The Department of Justice is prosecuting hypocrites who weaponized the justice system like Letitia James, the New York Attorney General who accused Trump of over-valuing his home Mar-a-Lago. No one has ever been punished with a $454 million penalty for a property valuation that the bank accepted and for a loan that was paid, yet the partisan

---

2. The U.S. pledge of allegiance, written by Francis Bellamy, a Christian and Baptist minister, in August 1892.

judge Arthur Engoron ordered Trump to pay. A New York appeals court threw out his judgment entirely. In a twist of irony, Letitia James was indicted on October 9, 2025 for bank fraud and making false statements to a financial institution, allegedly underreporting assets to secure a lower interest loan. There is poetic justice.

Yes, under Trump, it seems justice has returned.

In the Prologue, I wrote: "Be careful about getting what you wish for." Trump may trigger the end of America by being too good at what he does. The whole world works with America because her leaders are full of corruption like everywhere else. They grease American politicians' wheels; U.S. leaders grease their wheels. They wink at each others' faults and flaws.

Trump threatens the whole system including the unelected Deep State, the European Union, the United Nations, and the World Health Organization. Believe George Soros when he says, "I find the current moment in history rather painful. Open societies are in crisis, and various forms of dictatorships and mafia states, exemplified by Putin's Russia, are on the rise. In the United States, President Trump would like to establish a mafia state but he can't..."[3] Believe Hillary Clinton when she says, "[Trump] is a direct threat to the national security of America."[4] Believe Barack Obama when he warned Trump in 2016, "The main advice that I give to the incoming president is the United States really is an indispensable nation in our world order."[5]

Whoever is running the world order is not feeling comfortable with Trump. Their entire system is being threatened not by a

---

3. https://www.georgesoros.com/2018/01/25/remarks-delivered-at-the-world-economic-forum/
4. https://www.pbs.org/newshour/show/hillary-clinton-trumps-actions-direct-threat-to-national-security. She also said, "Donald Trump's ideas are not just different, they are dangerously incoherent," in a June 03, 2016 speech against her rival. https://www.ndtv.com/world-news/hillary-clinton-attacks-trumps-foreign-policy-as-a-threat-to-us-safety-1415331
5. https://www.ndtv.com/world-news/barack-obama-warns-trump-that-us-underpins-world-order-1627986

Russian-colluding, Nazi-sympathizing Dictator. Those hoaxes have already been debunked. The system is being threatened by a righteous and just President.

There's a Scripture that seems odd, but makes sense here:

> **Ecclesiastes 7:16-17**
>
> **16** Be not overly righteous, and do not make yourself too wise. Why should you destroy yourself?
>
> **17** Be not overly wicked, neither be a fool. Why should you die before your time?

Trump may become a victim of his own success. He can pull sway over any nation because America is great. Wisdom says you should reserve this "tough guy" approach for bullies like Hamas, Iran, and narco terrorists.

Trump should not use the same approach with Russia and China. If they are all outed, they will do anything to save their skin. If they team up against America, the US grid can go down, the USD can be replaced, and America can become a victim of its own success.

Letting Russia and China enjoy their own success means they leave us alone. It doesn't mean they're good guys. It doesn't mean we're afraid of them. But creating enemies unnecessarily worldwide only draws them together. Alone, they cannot challenge America. But together, they can devise a plan to undermine the States, and they won't likely wait for Trump's term to be over. To them, it might be too late.

I say this because it's already happening. I'm not giving away a game plan to harm America that nobody knows. This is being spoken in the secret chambers where there are no cellphones.

THE 3 CROSSES OVER AMERICA THE SPOTS

Three solar eclipses crisscrossed the continental United States on 21 August 2017 (a total solar eclipse), 14 October 2023 (a partial), and 8 April 2024 (a total). Together three of them spell the first letter of the Hebrew alphabet: *aleph*. Two of them spell the last letter of the Hebrew alphabet: *tav* (equivalent of our T, which is why our "t" also looks like a cross). I believe they speak of 3 different types of judgment to come on 3 different locations.

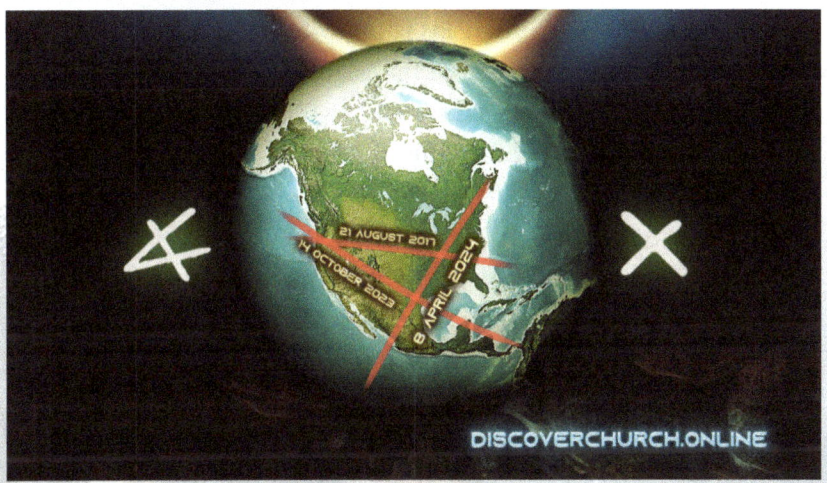

© 2025 by Steve Cioccolanti. The 3 Great American Solar Eclipses

I stood in Houston, Texas, proclaiming to Americans attending a prophecy conference that America's last warning had come: the Great American solar eclipse of August 21, 2017. Days later from the 25th-29th, Hurricane Harvey devastated southern Texas. Even though we were not on the path of totality, the Lord had sent me as a prophet to stand at the epicenter of the devastation. That's when I learned three things.

THE SIGN

First, I learned an appreciation for the prophet Isaiah's words:

> **Isaiah 8:18** (KJV)
> Behold, I and the children whom the LORD hath given me are for signs and for wonders in Israel from the LORD of hosts, which dwelleth in mount Zion.

Sometimes all the Lord needs is for us to stand there. We are the sign. Before people could hear a message about eclipses, my arrival (out of all the places on earth I could be) signals an invitation or a warning. Jesus' words confirm this:

> **Matthew 10:41**
> The one who receives a prophet because he is a prophet will receive a prophet's reward, and the one who receives a righteous person because he is a righteous person will receive a righteous person's reward.

The prophet's reward in Jonah's case was extended mercy. Nineveh survived another 120 years from 760 BC to 640 BC. The prophet's reward in Nahum's case was justice. Nineveh was destroyed after his final warning. Jesus again confirmed that Jonah himself was the sign, not merely his sermon:

> **Luke 11:30**
> For as Jonah became a sign to the Ninevites, so also the Son of Man will be to this generation.

Jesus is telling us that we should be looking to the Book of Jonah in the end times. What happened there?

THE SIGN OF JONAH

Jonah was not a model preacher. He was not willing to obey right away. He was a reluctant prophet who ran away from his destiny. He didn't particularly want Nineveh to be saved. Nothing in the story indicates he was the Billy Graham of his day. He probably didn't start with great jokes, tell great stories, or share interesting analogies. Why did people respond so well to Jonah and repented en masse so quickly?

Because they had been prepared by at least 4 signs. God said, *"Go and preach in Nineveh"* (Jonah 1:2 & 3:2). Before Jonah arrived, the following signs were recorded in history:

- A plague visited their city in 765 BC
- The Assyrian Solar Eclipse or Bur-Sagale Eclipse crossed directly over their city in 763 BC
- A plague returned in 760 BC
- Then the earthquake of Amos 1:1 shook the city in 760 BC.

The people of Nineveh did not worship the God of the Bible, but they had some spiritual sense. They connected the dots and said, *"This is not good for us. These are omens…signs of pending judgment."* Then the prophet Jonah came. Do you have the context now? Jonah wasn't just a great preacher. He wasn't so eloquent that he convinced them all. They were a *prepared* people because of these signs, and then the Bible says:

> **Jonah 3:4** (NKJV)
> "Yet forty days [you get 40 more days], and Nineveh shall be overthrown!"

Based on this sign, I predicted a tragedy would occur in America or the Middle East. I did not know what it was, but I was sure it'd come 40 days after April 8, 2024. I said in my meetings at David Herzog's His Glory Zone in Chandler, Arizona.

April 8 + 40 days = May 18/the eve of Pentecost

Christians stopped paying attention to the Heavens because they were afraid that it's like astrology, where you look at the stars to tell you your future. The difference for Bible prophecy watchers is that these signs are written in the sky by the Creator to point to Himself, not to us! When a sign lines up with the Hebrew calendar or the Christian calendar, we believe this is not mere coincidence—these 3 eclipses are a final warning for the United States. We're not getting any more signs like these in our lifetime. This is it. God loves America very much, because not every nation gets a sign written in the sky over their land. This is our biggest warning.

On May 18, 2024, there was a unique event. The President of Iran Ebrahim Raisi was killed in freak helicopter crash. I believe he was assassinated, 40 days after the last solar eclipse. Some reported that the weather map of that specific day has been wiped off the records. Why?

This death somehow ties America's future to Iran. We will have to keep dealing with Iran till the end. 440 days after the final eclipse warning, on June 22, 2025, Trump dropped 14 bunker busting bombs (MOPs) on Iran and ended their regime's mockery of Israel (for the time being). 400 and 40 are both cycles of trial, as explained in *The Divine Code*. 440 is a period of testing. Trump waited patiently for Iran to accept peace, they would not. 14 is the number of salvation (for Israel).

The redemption process always starts with a plague. Just as Egypt was a struck with a plague, and Nineveh was struck with a plague, so too America was struck with the COVID pandemic. This was the first wake up call—the White Horse has started running.

The sign of Jonah was much more than Jonah being "swallowed up by a whale" (which was not a whale, but a great sea monster). It began with a plague, continued with a solar eclipse, and ended with a great quake. When Jonah showed up, the people had been well prepared. I am showing you the signs so that when God sends you a Jonah, you can believe quickly and repent quickly.

THE PROPHET PRECEDES JUSTICE

The second lesson I learned was that God would not send judgment till He sends a prophet. Who knows how many people Jonah met in Nineveh. Who knows if he preached on the streets or in the royal palace. What's important was that the prophet arrived, and the book of Jonah goes to great pains to get the prophet there. A great sea monster had to swallow the reluctant prophet and spit him out at the right port along the Mediterranean coast so that Jonah would arrive at the right place at the right time.

When Nineveh received Jonah, the judgment was stayed. And when Nineveh forgot God and tried His patience 120 years later, He didn't bring judgment without sending a prophet. This time he sent Nahum. God is unwilling to do anything till a prophet arrives, sometimes at the cost of his own life.

The Lord would send my children and me to place after place, and before I ever preached, we were a sign. I was sent to Maui before the Maui fire. I was sent to Los Angeles where I prophesied in Kim Clement's studio to get out before the two Los Angeles fires of September 29-October 5, 2017, and of January 7-31, 2025. L.A. Marzulli's house burned down in the first fire and he lost many of his precious artifacts he had collected concerning the Nephilim. After that loss, he moved to Oklahoma. The Clements moved to Tenessee.

It pays to receive a prophet in the name of a prophet. God is trying to save lives whether the judgment can or cannot be stopped. The Body of Christ will have to learn how to honor the prophet's office to be able to escape in time. Sometimes the prophet doesn't spell out everything; sometimes his presence is enough. We have to "read between the lines."

The tragedy of Texas was that there were mega churches everywhere, but not one of the mega church pastors were interested in hearing about the Great American solar eclipse in 2017. Invitations were sent, but the local pastor said not one of them were interested. Not one welcomed me. Those churches were judged by God during COVID, when they lost members, money and/or their ministries.

After COVID, I was sent to visit Gateway Church in the Southlake suburb of Dallas. Pastor Robert Morris did not meet me, but his executive pastor did. I told him I had met Pastor Morris in a pastors' conference in Japan several years earlier. As a young pastor, I offered him a new perspective on his doctrine on tithing, and to my pleasant surprise, he publicly corrected what he taught and said verbatim what I told him, "Tithing is NOT the first. Firstfruits is the first, tithing is the tenth."

I was impressed with his massive church—he must be a highly skilled leader. But most of all I thought the LORD had sent me there for a reason, but I didn't yet know what. I left my phone number and email and, typical of churches, they say, "Let's keep in touch," but they don't. They become too busy to discern the will of God. In June 2024, Pastor Morris admitted to sexually abusing a 12-year-old girl, Cindy Clemishire, over four years in the 1980s.

I don't want to scare you from meeting me, because I am sent everywhere to be a blessing. It's how you receive a prophet that determines your reward. I am not bringing you judgment. People who reject me aren't cursed. Please understand: I don't cause any judgment on anyone; the Lord sends me at the right time to help people, and He sometimes uses me as a sign to warn people to avert judgment. I am usually the last one in a long string of warnings. The Lord trusts me not always to be first, but to be last.

Another time I was sent to Asia to meet a wealthy businesswoman and tell her to put God first and be careful about her motives. We must not only do what looks right to the government or to fellow Christian, but do it with purity. We should not hide anything. I told her these specific words, "Wherever I go, I come with blessings. But according to a pattern I've noticed over many years, I am often the last person that people will meet before judgment."

She did not understand what I was saying and two weeks later, her boyfriend (a man she lived with but didn't marry as a way to protect both their financial assets) slipped in a bathtub and died. She started focusing on the Lord's business and stopped living in sin. She is a great servant of God today.

THE MYSTERY OF PROPHECY

The third lesson I learned was that the prophet often does not fully understand his own message. The Lord will not give it all to him. Partly it's to keep him humble. Partly it's to prove to listeners that the prophet didn't make it up with his own reasoning; God is the One working far beyond our minds.

Six years after my message to Houston, I moved to America and preached from state to state, warning believers about the next two American solar eclipses. Only when the second eclipse of October 14, 2023 came did I realize Houston had been marked out ahead of time by the path of annularity.

The partial solar eclipse entered the continent from Oregon and exited through Texas, crossing Houston perfectly. It took 6 years for the prophet who proclaimed it to figure it out. Truly God's Word is beyond our capacity to doctor or engineer.

The 2023 eclipse entered the continent through:

- **Salem**, Oregon (same word as *Shalom*, which is also in the name Jerusalem), crossed
- **Goshen**, Utah (a key concept the Lord would give me for the Black Horse), crossed

- **Jonah**, Texas (the sign), before moving southeast to
- **Houston**, Texas (where the Flood had come 6 years earlier).

God saw 2023 since 2017. I had to wait to 2023 to see 2017 in clear light. Now in 2025, I see more again. We must learn to be patient about prophecy—Glory to God!

For comparison, the 2017 eclipse crossed these towns with Biblical allusion:

- **Salem**, Oregon ("Salem" tied to Jerusalem)
- **Bethany**, Missouri (New Testament village of Lazarus, Mary and Martha; the place where Lazarus was buried and resurrected; likely the place where Jesus concluded His earthly ministry and ascended to Heaven; also the middle name of my firstborn)
- **Jerusalem**, Arkansas (the Holy City of Peace)
- **Bethlehem**, Georgia (Jesus' birthplace)

The point of exit, Bethlehem, suggested the sign did not signal the end, but the beginning of the birth pangs. In 2023, we had just witnessed the first seal broken and the first Horsemen riding.

Then on April 8, 2024 came the biggest sign of them all. It crossed 11 Ninevehs in North America, along with some other significant towns, notably "Rapture"!

- **Jonah**, Texas
- **Nineveh**, Texas
- **Jerusalem**, Arkansas
- **Nineveh**, Missouri
- **Little Egypt**, Illinois
- **Rapture**, Indiana
- **Nineveh**, Indiana
- **Ninevah**, Kentucky (misspelling of Nineveh)

- **Nineveh**, Ohio
- **Nineveh**, Pennsylvania
- **Nineveh**, Pennsylvania
- **Nineveh**, Virginia
- **Nineveh**, New York
- **Nineveh**, Nova Scotia
- **Nineveh**, Nova Scotia

All Ninevehs in America are under the path of this eclipse! Nineveh was the city to which Jonah was sent to deliver a final warning. Jesus said Jonah would be an end time sign: "This is an evil generation. It seeks a sign, and no sign will be given to it except the sign of Jonah the prophet." (Luke 11:29) Eleven is the number of chaos, as explained in my book *The Divine Code: A Prophetic Encyclopedia of Numbers*.

How fitting 11 Ninevehs were marked out, along with Jonah at the start and Rapture right after the eclipse left Little Egypt. We will leave this world (Egypt) via the Rapture in while the birth pangs continue to usher in the Messiah.

There's a lot more to the signs. They're simply amazing. The three solar eclipses of 2017-2024 make intersections or form three crosses.

The first cross is over Texas, where Hurricane Harvey floods came in August 2017, and the strange Texas Panhandle fires came on February 26-28, 2025.

But the "X" formed by the 2023 and 2024 eclipses marked a specific town named Kerrville, Texas. If you didn't know before that these were the Great American Signs of the End Times, you should have known that day. Kerrville experienced a rare and deadly flash flood on July 4th, 2025—America's Independence Day.

Texas has been judged severely, several times, because it is the most Christian of the states on the paths of the eclipses. Peter said, "For the time is come that judgment must begin at the house of God" (1 Peter 4:17).

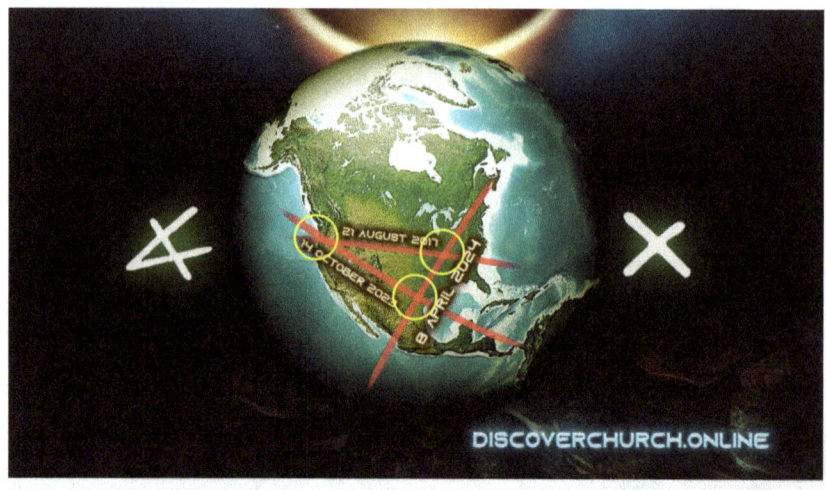

© 2025 by Steve Cioccolanti. Triple Intersection of 3 Solar Eclipse Paths

TRIPLE INTERSECTION POINTS OF THE SOLAR ECLIPSE PATHS

- 1st cross over **Kerrville, Texas**. X formed by the 2023 and 2024 eclipses.
- 2nd cross over **Salem, Oregon**. X formed by the 2017 and 2023 eclipses.
- 3rd cross over **Little Egypt, Illinois**. X formed by the 2017 and 2024 eclipses. Little Egypt actually sits on the northern tip of the New Madrid Seismic Zone (NMSZ), which is where the focal point of judgment will be.

Just as surely as Texas received judgment, Oregon and the NMSZ will be next. I believe a great quake (6.0+) in the NMSZ will divide America. It will interrupt the trade routes of both the Mississippi River and Interstate Route 55. The quake will cause liquefaction, reverse the flow of the Mississippi River, and stop or slow the 500 million tons of freight that depend on these passageways annually.

The quake would be followed by a shortage of food, water and medical supplies.

When these happen, those who are "watching and praying" will fear God more and obey Him more quickly, for the time is short. God commands all men everywhere to repent and trust His Son (Acts 17:30). Pray this prayer to get right with God:

> *Dear Heavenly Father, I'm sorry I'm a sinner. I ask You to forgive me before it's too late. I place my total faith and complete trust in Jesus Christ Your Son to save me. I cannot save myself. I believe He died for me on the cross, He paid for my sins, and He rose again from the dead. He is alive! Come live in me. From this day forward, my life is not my own. I belong to You. I have been bought with a price. Prepare me to be a worthy child of God. Use me as You please, in Jesus' Name I pray. Amen.*

Congratulations! This is the first step to being ready for the coming King. You are forgiven and accepted into God's Family through Jesus' sacrifice. You are a child of God. Live like it!

You will need to learn about divine health and healing as soon as possible. Remember the sign of Jonah was a series of events. The *Bur-Sagale* solar eclipse of 763 BC was preceded by a plague and then followed by a plague. I believe that's exactly what's going to happen. Another plague worse than COVID is coming. You will need to know God as Your Healer.

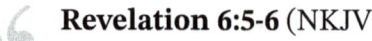

CHAPTER 13
THE BLACK HORSE

3ᴿᴰ SEAL: **The Black Horse**

> **Revelation 6:5-6** (NKJV)
> **5** When He opened the third seal, I heard the third living creature say, "Come and see." So I looked, and behold, a black horse, and he who sat on it had a pair of scales in his hand [an essential tool used to measure both commodities and currencies till recent times; a reference to commerce and the economy].
> **6** And I heard a voice in the midst of the four living creatures saying, "A quart of wheat for a denarius [a day's wage for a soldier], and three quarts of barley for a denarius; and do not harm the oil and the wine."

The Black Horse refers to an economic recession or depression that's going to be accompanied by global famine. It will be triggered by a Black Swan[1] event, hence the "Black" Horse. Many economists have been predicting the next stock market crash, real estate crash, dollar collapse, crypto adoption, and CBDC implementation. Most of them got the timing wrong. The Black Horse gives us a definite timeframe.

American investor and libertarian philosopher Doug Casey seems to have his finger on the pulse. I don't think he's getting his info from the Bible, but his research serves as independent corroboration of what I'm predicting. On 14 October 2025, his team contributor Jeff Thomas posted *Where Not to Be in a Crisis*:

> *All of the traditional warning signs are present, and although technology has changed considerably over the millennia, human behavior has not. We are witnessing the same symptoms that were present in major collapses of the past, going back at least as far as the Roman Empire.*
>
> *We are therefore seeing not only the initial stages of an economic collapse but the concurrent events, such as an almost total corruption of the political structure, a move toward totalitarian rule, the destruction of currencies, and a loss of faith in leadership across the board. Along the way, we're also experiencing a decline in logic and morality and an eroding sense of humanity.*
>
> *That's quite a lot to take in, yet, sorry to say; we're only in the first stages of collapse. It will get quite a bit worse before it gets better.*[2]

When the 3rd Seal is broken and the Black Horse is unleashed,

---

1. A term coined by Nassim Nicholas Taleb in his 2007 book *The Black Swan: The Impact of the Highly Improbable*.
2. https://internationalman.com/articles/where-not-to-be-in-a-crisis/

one loaf of bread is going to cost you your entire day's wage. The NET translates it as: "A loaf of wheat bread or three loaves of barley will cost a day's pay." That indicates hyperinflation. Let's give you a prelude in different currencies:

Country | Maximum[3] Cost of One Meal
U.S.A. | $250
U.K. | £150
Australia | AUD185
Singapore | SGD330
Japan | ¥7,700

What would cause this? When will it happen? Will the USD collapse? We are given many clues about what the Black Horse is.

---

3. I say "maximum" not to exaggerate the prophecy or overly scare you because a denarius bought far less in Roman times than a day's wage would buy now. This is due to the efficiency of capitalism that began in Christian countries (not in any pagan country): the scientific revolution is a direct effect of belief in an intelligent God who orders the universe with discoverable laws; the business revolution is a direct effect of belief that God holds us accountable to treat others with honesty, integrity and without coercion (the foundation of capitalism) and God grants us inalienable rights such as the right to life, liberty and personal property, including intellectual property; Christian leaders also promoted literacy (mainly to read the Bible) and abolished slavery (Abraham Lincoln in the U.S., William Wilberforce in the U.K.) leading to greater equality in opportunities, incomes and lifestyles.

By contrast, the Romans had impressive engineering (aqueducts, roads, theaters) and commerce, but ordinary citizens faced high disease, malnutrition, and inequality. Economic growth was limited by rampant immorality, corruption, slave labor, low productivity and only sporadic innovation.

The Protestant Reformation (1517) and subsequent Great Awakening in America (1720-40) broke through the constraints of ancient economies, sparked progress in industry (First Industrial Revolution, 1760-1830; Second, 1870-1914) and sustained it by instilling the "Protestant work ethic." This is why America, the most Christian country on earth, is also the richest. If America stays Christian, it should minimize the effects of recession.

BLACK

"Black" obviously represents one thing in the world economy: "petroleum" (crude oil), from which we refine "gas" in America, or "petrol" in the rest of the world. It's also called "Black Gold." Petrol influences the price of everything, because everything needs to be transported to us.

Rather than trying to control separate commodities and industries, the globalists can crash the economy by causing oil price to spike. What does this achieve? A great many things:

- They can blame Trump for a recession or depression.
- When the price of everything becomes expensive, people will be upset and vote for "hope and change."
- Globalists will gain back control of the U.S. House and Senate in November 2026. The Trump agenda (protection of free speech, more peace, fewer wars, more jobs, less crimes, border protection, promotion of Christian values) will be dead at the door.
- A crash discredits capitalism, paving the way to "build back better" with green socialism, where elites profit from new industries (EVs, carbon credits) while suppressing dissent. Klaus Schwab calls this "stakeholder capitalism."[4] American professor and author Michael Rectenwald calls it "corporate capitalism."[5] Italian philosopher Giorgio Agamben called it "communist capitalism."[6]
- Every crash is a fire sale. It allows the elites to buy

---

4. Klaus Schwab and Peter Vanham, *Stakeholder Capitalism: A Global Economy that Works for Progress, People and Planet* (Hoboken, NJ: Wiley, 2021).
5. Michael Rectenwald, *The Great Reset, Part II: Corporate Socialism*, Mises Wire, December 26, 2020.
6. Giorgio Agamben, *Capitalismo comunista*, Quodlibet, December 15, 2020.

distressed assets (stocks, real estate, businesses, bitcoin). They want a global sale, not merely a local sale.
- Colonization of non-Western nations. A controlled demolition of the economy allows Western powers to weaken fossil-fuel-dependent nations and force their reliance on globalist-controlled alternatives (renewables). Many nations remain highly dependent on fossil fuel in their economies, including some wealthy Middle Eastern ones.
- Economic despair justifies emergency measures, eroding freedoms, isolating individuals, and making them more dependent on government ("you will own nothing and be happy"[7]). **Hannah Arendt** (1906-1975), an expert on totalitarianism, called it **"organized loneliness"** but on a scale never seen before.[8] The premise is simple: To centralize control over currencies, borders and resources, people have to obey. Totalitarians achieve this by deliberate social engineering tactics: atomizing individuals, stripping away communal bonds (church and family), punishing men and fatherhood (the patriarchy), rewarding single motherhood and "single households," imposing loneliness through terror, propaganda and bureaucracy. Communists can make people feel alone even in crowds, as people's minds become rooted in fear, suspicion and ideological conformity.
- Implement the Great Reset by controlling the price of oil.

Ultimately, the anti-Christ elites need an energy crisis to force reliance on their Green alternatives (renewables). President Trump

---

7. World Economic Forum, *8 Predictions for the World in 2030* (video), 2016, https://www.facebook.com/worldeconomicforum/videos/10153920524981479
8. https://journalofethics.ama-assn.org/article/health-and-loneliness/2023-11

has thus far prevented them from executing their plan for global dominance, which we will look at in the Green Horse chapter.

WHY CRASH THE ECONOMY?

A spike in the price of oil would lead to an energy crisis, which leads to the 4th Horse—the Green. The globalists want to switch to green; people's freedom and Trump's leadership stand in the way.

Consumers have a choice currently. They are not all switching to globalist-controlled energy alternatives, such as buying solar panels and connecting them to a centralized solar grid. Integrated solar panels present risk: they don't work during cloudy days and wintery days; being connected to a super grid amplifies failure and cascading outages (one fails, all fails); and they can be switched off (not your choice).

Oil and gas are cheap and abundant. If I cook my food with my own gas tank, it doesn't matter if electricity goes out somewhere else. I still have cheap, reliable energy. To counter this in Victoria, Australia, the globalist Labor government has made it illegal to install gas to new homes. They are preparing for the Black Horse to lead to the Green Horse.

WHAT TO EXPECT

Here are the clues given by the Book of Revelation:

Black = the color of Oil, Petroleum, Gas. This refers to a great price spike in gas. Once gas goes up (as we saw during the pandemic), the price of everything else goes up because fossil fuels transport it. So, we've got inflation coming—even hyperinflation.

Note, some theologians and academics claim that "oil" must always refer to "olive oil" in the Bible. This is a childish way of looking at prophecy. Firstly, the color "black" must be harmonized with the "oil" in the same passage. There is no edible black olive oil, but there is plenty of combustible black oil. Secondly, God uses double entendres and plays-on-words all the time. I teach this principle when I teach on Bible Interpretation. Search our online store for many videos on this subject: www.Discover-Church.Online/shop

Black = Black Swan. As mentioned, black can also refer to a "Black Swan" event—an extremely rare, unpredictable, high-impact event. The name comes from the old European belief that all swans are white, until black swans were discovered in Australia, shattering the assumption. I have personally lived through at least 8 Black Swan events:

- 1991: The fall of the Soviet Union due to the prayers of the saints under communism and the appearance of a strong conservative leader, President Ronald Reagan. The sudden collapse ended the Cold War and redrew the world map, setting millions free from communism.
- 1993: The rise of the internet. I was one of the first people to get an email account from my university. Few predicted how fast the internet would transform commerce, communication and media.
- 2001: The September 11 Terrorist Attacks on America. There was no precedent for using planes as weapons at that scale.
- 2008: The Global Financial Crisis (GFC). U.S. housing prices collapsed after reaching peak in 2006. Subprime lenders collapse in 2007 gave early signs of a housing bubble starting to deflate. Lehman Brothers' collapse on September 15, 2008 was "impossible" (too big to fail) per financial experts. It was followed by Iceland's bank collapse in October 2008 (3 banks defaulted within days of each other; the largest systemic banking failure in history); followed by Greece's sovereign debt default in 2012. The GFC directly led to the next Black Swan.
- 2009: Bitcoin's creation, now a $1 trillion asset.

- 2011: The Tohoku Earthquake, Tsunami and Fukushima Nuclear Reactor Meltdown combo. A "1-in-1000-year" combo.
- 2016: Donald Trump elected President of the United States. Every poll projected a loss for Trump.
- 2020: COVID-19 Pandemic. The novel coronavirus caused global shutdowns on an unprecedented scale.

We will soon see a 9th Black Swan that will trigger the Black Horse (December 2026—January 2027). France is overextended in debt and unlike the U.S., does not have the world's reserve currency to prop up its economy. China is poised to strike at America's infrastructure. North Korea and Iran are unpredictable.

Russia is being pushed by NATO to "start" a wider war during the Red Horse. Putin's likeliest target would be Poland. A date for this was given in a dream: "**10/26**," which by international standard points to October 2026. When you see this happen, the instruction is to flee to a safe place (see the next chapter). Watch: The OCTOBER SURPRISE Prophecy.

The most poetic fulfillment of the Black Horse would be a repeat of the **Tulip Mania** of 1636-37. As explained in my video, "WHEN the USD Collapses | The TULIP Mania PROPHECY - Christians Were Never Told This!" tulips did not originate from the Netherlands. They came from a region stretching eastward from modern Turkey all the way to modern Iran. Guess what?

Ezekiel 38:2-6 talks about Iran (*Persia*) and Turkey (*Meshech, Tubal, Gomer, Beth Togarmah*) being the leaders of an invasion of Israel. Just as they triggered the collapse of 1636-37, they could trigger the collapse of 2026-27. It would not surprise me that Iran and Turkey would play a central role in another GFC, and that France and Germany would trigger another war.

| Tulip Mania Prophecy

The darkest prediction I wish I did not have to make is the loss of Donald Trump. On August 28, 2025, the Lord gave me a vivid dream of meeting President Trump in the Middle East. He was giving me an exclusive interview. He told me at the end of the year, he will no longer be President. He seemed content about it.[9]

Trump surviving an assassination attempt at Butler, Pennsylvania, on July 13, 2024

On October 20, 2025, the leftist environmental activist President of Colombia Gustavo Petro threatened to overthrow Trump. In an interview with Univision News, Petro snapped his fingers and said "get rid of Trump!"[10]

Trump is winning economically in his second term, yet accordingly to the timeline we've been given by the Book of Revelation, Christians will get only 2 years of this pro-Christian, pro-Israel agenda. This means we either lose Trump and/or lose the House and Senate at the November 3rd, 2026 Congressional midterm elections. When this happens, the Church at large will not be prepared for what's coming next.

The Church's response to Trump's success has been tepid.

---

9. "The TRUMP DREAM 2025," on YouTube, uploaded August 31, 2025: https://www.youtube.com/watch?v=vjjRfHxRrgQ

10. https://www.youtube.com/watch?v=D5zv92zEXwE

President Trump appointed 3 conservative justices that allowed the Supreme Court to overturn *Roe v. Wade*. This is what Christians have been praying for: the reversal of the legalization of abortion. It's been the biggest issue the Church has prayed against for 5 decades. Trump handed the Church one of the biggest moral victories in U.S. history. How many pastors celebrated or even mentioned Trump in good light after this prayer answer? Too few.

President Trump negotiated the release of the last surviving hostages of the October 7, 2023 Terror Attack. Hamas agreed and released all 20 on October 13, 2025. This is the role of a Christian leader: to be an agent of justice on the earth. No one else could do it. Trump did it. Churches should have been throwing parties for this achievement. Did they? Did yours?

If the Church did not celebrate two undeniable victories for Christians and Jews, do we deserve to enjoy 8 years of Trump? We don't deserve him. Since the Church does not appreciate enough what the Lord has done through Trump, we will almost certainly lose him. It's a Biblical principle: whatever we're ungrateful of we tend to lose.

The Lord asked me to document *"President Trump's Pro-Christian Accomplishments"* in a book by the same name. After January 6th, 2020, Google memory-holed many of my citations (the links are broken). It is truly a shame that many Christians still don't know how much God did through this one man.

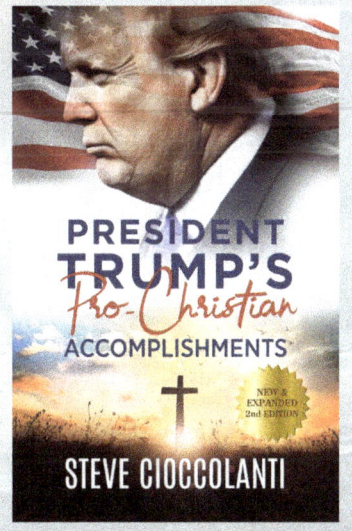

It seems to me that as long as Trump is present, the globalist oligarchs are unlikely to implement their plan to enslave humanity. The fear level necessary for "emergency powers" has dropped significantly because of Trump. Some who hear my message say, "The Church must pray for him to make it through all 8 years." I agree—I hope she does. I hope this prophetic alarm wakes up half of the Sleeping Virgins (or unprepared, lukewarm Christians as per Matthew 25).

Pair of Scales = Commerce, Trade, the Economy. This reminds me of Proverbs 11:1 (NKJV), "Dishonest scales are an abomination to the Lord, But a just weight is His delight." The elites use dishonest scales. The printing of money with no asset backing in the real world is an instance of dishonest scales.

It also reminds me of Daniel's prophecy to Belshazzar, "MENE: God has numbered your kingdom, and finished it; TEKEL: You have been weighed in the balances, and found wanting; PERES: Your kingdom has been divided and give to [another]." (Daniel 5:26-28) That very night Belshazzar was slain.

Dishonest statistics will be a prominent feature of the era of the Black Horse.

Expensive Bread = Inflation, Food Shortage, Famine. On top of hyperinflation, the Black Horse will bring food shortages. We saw a bit of it due to supply chain disruption during COVID: shelves were empty of toilet paper, eggs and other essentials off and on during 2020-2023. I also noticed how quickly a food-producing nation like Sri Lanka fell into famine in 2022. How did it happen?

Colonialism had made Sri Lanka dependent on growing tea to export to global consumers, rather than producing a diverse array of crops for its own citizens. Globalists then made Sri Lanka dependent on foreign synthetic fertilizers (45-50% from China, 15-20% India, 10-12% Qatar, Russia 8-10%—this is veritably a list of the "usual suspects" behind many global conflicts in the last days).

In April 2021, in an effort to reverse Sri Lanka's dependence on globalist synthetics and promote "100% organic farming," President Gotabaya Rajapaksa's government banned imports of chemical fertilizers and pesticides. Rice production immediately dropped. Simultaneously, the government banned some food imports and rationed fuel. This shortage of fuel caused water shortage. Fuel rationing (in 2022) also halted irrigation pumps and harvest transport. Vegetable and rice yields rotted in the fields. Rice, wheat, lentils, and dairy became unaffordable, with prices surging 50–100%.

Man-made famine was triggered and riots ensued. President Gotabaya Rajapaksa did the right thing but too fast. He was like a Sri Lankan version of RFK Jr. who needed a Trump to work alongside him. RFK Jr. ran for president in 2020 but would not have made a good president; he made a good Secretary of Health and Human Services (HHS). People need to team up to achieve more. Change must be implemented measure by measure, especially when it concerns food. President Rajapaksa wanted to remove synthetic fertilizers; it should have been done slowly. Even God would not remove enemies from the Promised Land in one shot.

> **Exodus 23:29-30**
> I will not drive them out from before you in one year, lest the land become desolate and the wild beasts multiply against you. **30** Little by little I will drive them out from before you, until you have increased and possess the land.

God created sovereign nations to protect against human error and ambition in other parts of the world. Nations are our safeguards against megalomaniacs like the ancient Nimrod, the builder of the Tower of Babel and the first globalist. **The goal of godly rulers is to make each country an independent, sovereign, self-sufficient state, able to repel foreign threats**.

The goal of evil rulers is to weaken sovereign states so they can be easily sliced up, manipulated and exploited by the ruling class. They do so in the name of "unity," "community," "compassion," and/or "safety." One of the greatest revelations that will help you understand globalism is that global elites prioritize their own interests and networks over national citizens. Their allegiance is more to each other (families and dynasties of the global oligarchy) than to their own citizens.

The only elite that might be the exception to this is a good king (or a President who acts like a father to the nation). Hence, Thailand's King Bhumibol Adulyadej (Rama IX) encouraged every Thai family to be self-sufficient by owning their own land and having their own food, water and income. He actively helped farmers become more productive with crops that yielded more in their region and climate.

He introduced the "four-part integrated farming system" designed for small landholders. Farmers were encouraged to produce 80–90% of their needs on-site, minimizing reliance on foreign markets or chemicals. You can imagine how this is anathema to the globalist oligarchy.

They cannot influence, bribe, control or buy off a king like they do politicians. This makes strong monarchies the enemies of colonizers and is why Americans constantly hear about how bad kings and kingdoms are. As Christians, we should question this narrative. Doesn't the Bible show God prefers kingdoms? He calls His Son Jesus a King, and Jesus calls us "kings." (Revelation 1:6, 5:10)

Let's get back to what to expect. A full-blown famine is not something Americans are used to. The Bible predicted it, so we have to prepare for it. We should get going with preparing long-life food[11], shelter, and safety (called a *Goshen*) before the Black Horse. The Red Horse is galloping now. The Black Horse is next.

Do not Harm the Oil and the Wine = ?

I put a question mark on this because like the "bow" and "crown" of the First Horse, I do not want to jump the gun; we may not fully know what the "wine" refers to till the Black Horse starts.

It could refer to "wine" in the most ordinary sense of the word:

---

11. I personally like two sources of long-life food from Christian suppliers, as noted in the Chapter *Goshen*.

a red drink made from fermented grapes. Noah, the Old Testament figure most related to global judgment, had a vineyard and drank wine soon after he was off the ark (Genesis 9:21). Why was this mentioned after the Global Flood, and mentioned again in the 3rd Seal?

We can prepare the Church by anticipating the word "wine" may not be understood in English. Here I will translate for you the word "wine" into the 3 languages written over Jesus' head when He was crucified on the Cross: Greek, Latin, and Hebrew.

- **Oinos** (Greek: οἶνος)
- **Yayin** (Hebrew, written right to left: יין)
- **Vinum** (Latin, from which we derive wine, vineyard, vinegar). In Spanish and Italian it is "*vino.*" In French and Romanian "*vin.*"

In ancient Greece, wine was associated with Dionysus, the god of wine/fertility/theater/ecstasy, symbolizing madness/chaos. That seems to align with the economic chaos of the 3rd Seal. This would mean partying, revelry and entertainment continue during the Black Horse.

The third word in question is "harm."

- The NIV, NASB, and NET translate the phrase as, "Do not damage...."
- The Good News Translation takes liberty to elaborate, "Do not damage the olive trees and the vineyards!" If that's correct then it means protection of agriculture during the Black Horse.
- The King James says, "See thou hurt not the oil and the wine."
- The NLT says, "Don't waste the olive oil and wine."

Don't waste has a different meaning than don't hurt, harm, or damage. Don't waste implies there is an abundance, not to be wasted or spent for no reason. Don't harm implies there is scarcity, so protect what's left. There is an interesting prediction in Sanhedrin 97a verses 24-25: "In the generation of Messiah's coming impudence will increase, esteem be perverted, the vine yield its fruit, yet shall wine be dear."[12] This suggests there is an abundance of wine, just as Revelation 6:6 predicts (don't waste it), but the price will skyrocket, just as Revelation 6:5 predicts (the scales come out to weigh the heavier price). We will soon find out the meanings of oil, wine and harm.

We know one thing for certain: God limits judgment. He told satan concerning Job, "Behold, he is in your hand [he deserves judgment]; only spare his life [he doesn't deserve death]." (Job 2:6)

In the 5th Shofar judgment, locusts will come out of the bottomless pit and be given power to sting like scorpions. "They were told not to harm the grass of the earth or any green plant or any tree, but only those people who do not have the seal of God on their foreheads." (Revelation 9:4) God spares the remaining plants (after a third of trees and grass were burned up at the 1st Shofar). Likewise, we know the rider of the Black Horse is restricted from wasting or harming certain commodities.

OIL AND WINE

While theologians debate whether "oil and wine" are luxury commodities for the elites or necessary foods for commoners during the time of the Black Horse, I have a third view.

What if the "oil and wine" that is preserved is for health? What if it refers to natural medicine or nutraceuticals? It would match the time people are living in and the troubles they're going through.

We have many Scriptures to confirm this. Jesus said the Good Samaritan took care of a stranger left half-dead on the side of the

---

12. https://halakhah.com/sanhedrin/sanhedrin_97.html

road: "He went to him and bound up his wounds, pouring on OIL and WINE." (Luke 10:34) Why would you put "oil and wine" on someone sick unless they were natural remedies? Paul advised Timothy, "No longer drink only water, but use a little wine for the sake of your stomach and your frequent ailments." (1 Timothy 5:23) Hippocrates, the father of medicine, used *oinos* (diluted wine) therapeutically for restoring health.[13]

Yes, you can allegorize almost anything in the Bible to search for a deeper meaning, but when it can make sense literally, we should take the words at face value as the first level of interpretation.

Bible Healing Oils

I can tell you the benefits of Bible healing oil I've used internally and externally. The right combination of oil, frankincense and myrrh can heal cuts, bruises, skin rashes, insect bites, body aches, headaches, tummy aches, even tooth-aches. It's quite amazing that people go to toxic drugs for relief when the right kind of oil will reduce inflammation or heal them. The very name "Christ" means the "Anointed One" or the "Oiled One." That's a Biblical clue that good oil is for healing.

During the Black Horse, there will be food shortages, but believers should have access to natural remedies, functional medicine, holistic foods—natural alternatives to toxic drugs. My family has seen many benefits from using "Bible

---

13. Hippocrates, *Hippocratic Writings*, translators J. Chadwick and W. N. Mann (London: Penguin Classics, 1978), 76.
    The text reads: "Wine [oinos] is fit for man in a wonderful way, provided it is taken with good sense, by the sick as well as the healthy."

healing oil"[14] and other neutraceuticals for our healing. We always mix faith in God with whatever natural product God allows us to have. There are many solutions for you and your family. Research them, listen to the Spirit, and you'll know what to do.

In the next chapter, we'll look at the safest places to be during WW3. Learn how to protect yourself and identify Goshens during the famine, persecution and plagues. You have a limited time to prepare as the Black Horse is due to gallop for 3.5 years starting around December 2026—January 2027.

> Irene: Thank you for your insights. I have been listening to you since President Trump was running in 2016 and what you were saying at that time persuaded me he was God's choice. You have been spot on.

---

14. My favorite formula of Bible healing oil can be found here: http://www.BibleHealingoil.com/pages/pastorsteve

CHAPTER 14
GOSHEN

GOSHEN IS a term that became popular, but has been misused, among "preppers" during the COVID-19 pandemic. Some prophecy watchers and freedom fighters started looking for farms, ranches or safe places to buy and hide themselves from the coming plagues, wars, inflation, persecution and authoritarianism that are predicted in the Book of Revelation. Is this concept Scriptural? Ancient rabbis paid close attention to Amos 4:7.

> **Amos 4:7**
> "I also withheld the rain from you when there were yet three months to the harvest; I would send rain on one city, and send no rain on another city; one field would have rain, and the field on which it did not rain would wither;

This Scripture tells us it won't be bad in every place. Some places escape. This gives us the concept of **"Goshen."** While Egypt experienced the 10 plagues, the Israelites were safe and untouched in the fertile land of Goshen. Exodus is a prototype of what to do in the End Times. We should find our own Goshen.

During COVID, I watched many Christians look for safety from the lockdowns and mandates. They were prompted by the right spirit, but then human reasoning got mixed into it. Many went out to rural places or foreign nations, and wasted a lot of money. Some bought farms and failed. One family bought a large property and succeeded in making an organic farm business for a while, then floods destroyed it twice. With compassion, I prayed for them. I thought, "Don't they know if it's been hit by two floods, it's not a Goshen?"

God in His mercy tried to correct sincere believers. The Bible doesn't say He calls every Christian to live on a farm or buy a ranch in the end times. People who've been living in the city all their lives are not going to turn into good farmers overnight or even over months. They're probably not going to survive on a farm at all. Many got burned-out from looking, investing in the wrong places and finally gave up on the idea of "Goshen."

Let me save you a lot of time, effort and possibly heartache. This chapter is for you. The Lord has sent me to 60 countries. He's shown me some criteria for a Goshen. Let's have a Biblical look at what a Goshen really is.

Joseph said this to his brothers after they found out he's the Prince of Egypt:

> **Genesis 45:10**
> You shall dwell in the land of Goshen, and you shall be near to me, you and your children, your children's children, your flocks and your herds, and all that you have.

The Hebrew word for "*Goshen*" means to "draw near."[1] It makes

---

1. Goshen is assumed to be an Egyptian name, so the Hebrew root may not be the etymology of the Egyptian word, but it doesn't matter to us. We want to know what God thinks about it and God uses Hebrew and likes plays on words.

sense. In Hebrew, Joseph would have said, "You will *goshen* me at *Goshen*."

WHAT IS A GOSHEN?

1. Goshen is a place to draw near to the man of God. You should grow closer to God at a Goshen. To put it in New Testament terms, if a Goshen doesn't have a church, it isn't a Goshen. It's a real estate project. You can call it that. Tell customers, "This is my real estate development," but don't use God's name to sell property. That's wrong. A Goshen must have a man of God there and it should help people draw near to God. In the Genesis account, 66 people wanted to be near to Joseph.

> **Genesis 47:6**
> The land of Egypt is before you. Have your father and brothers dwell in the best of the land; let them dwell in the land of Goshen. And if you know any competent men among them, then make them chief herdsmen over my livestock."

2. A Goshen is the best of the land. It should have good soil, sun, water and fresh air.
3. Goshen is a place of community where competent men work together and share responsibilities. You cannot survive alone, no matter how much food or weaponry you have. A Goshen requires skilled people to help and protect each other in community. The Israeli *kibbutz* emphasizes this idea.

> **Genesis 47:27**
> So Israel dwelt in the land of Egypt, in the country

of Goshen; and they had possessions there and grew and multiplied exceedingly.

4. Goshen is a place for you to grow and multiply. The Bible does not paint a picture of Goshen being remote, isolated and rural. Goshen was not in the cities of Egypt, but neither was it a rural farm. At Goshen, 66 people who came from Canaan and 4 who were already there (Joseph, his wife, and their two sons) multiplied to 603,550 men or 3 million people. I've been to and/or led Christians on Biblical tours to Israel, Jordan, Turkey, Greece, and Italy. I can tell you that even a major capital city like ancient Rome had about 250,000 adult male citizens at the time of Jesus, giving it a total population of about 1 million maximum 2000 years ago. Ephesus, one of the most important ancient port cities in the Roman Empire, had 250,000 at maximum. Jerusalem had a population of 50,000 to 100,000 people at maximum. By comparison, most Bible schools teach that 3 million Jews escaped out of Egypt. Since they all lived in Goshen, that would have made it one of the most densely populated areas of the ancient world. Yes, it had farmland for sheep, but it was also full of people. Our modern idea of a "Goshen" needs to be updated according to the Bible.

> **Exodus 8:22, 9:26**
> And in that day I will set apart the land of Goshen, in which My people dwell, that no swarms of flies shall be there, in order that you may know that I am the Lord in the midst of the land...Only in the land of Goshen, where the children of Israel were, there was no hail.

5. Goshen means a safe place. None of the 10 plagues that affected the Egyptians touched the Israelites, including disease, climate change, and spiritual attacks. (Notice, climate change is nothing new. It was part of the 10 plagues, and no one blamed fossil fuels, cars, or carbon footprint.) A place of safety must have enough food, water, energy and clean air. It should not be a "hot spot" where wars or natural disasters are happening. It should be protected from political instability, famine, nuclear war, etc.

6. Goshen is a transitional place. I add this because the Israelites eventually moved out of Goshen. All Goshens are temporary. You go there to grow. You don't have to worry about whether you like your Goshen a lot—it doesn't really matter. You're to go draw near to a man of God, serve God, and be safe from the plagues. Once you've grown, you can move on. Growing may include finding your mate and building your family. A Goshen is not a single-sex monastery. It's not a place to hide away from normal socialization.

7. Goshen is the place for you to win souls and fulfill the Great Commission. By the time the Israelites left Goshen, a "mixed multitude" had joined them. That means they were winning converts there. God may use persecution to lead you out of your comfort zone and into an unevangelized area that is safe for you. That's a Goshen.

Now that we've studied the Bible's description of Goshen, let's see what a well-traveled, secular relocation expert considers criteria for safe places during WW3. Then, I will share with you my criteria and answer some objections and questions.

Jeff Thomas is a British investor and contributor to the

"International Man" founded by Doug Casey. He posted the following article, *Where Not to Be in Crisis*:

> *For many years, there have been those who have been prognosticating an economic crisis – not just a recession lasting a year or two, but a full-blown Greater Depression that would eclipse any major event we've seen in our lifetimes...*
>
> *All of the traditional warning signs are present, and although technology has changed considerably over the millennia, human behaviour has not. We are witnessing the same symptoms that were present in major collapses of the past, going back at least as far as the Roman Empire.*
>
> *We are therefore seeing not only the initial stages of an economic collapse but the concurrent events, such as an almost total corruption of the political structure, a move toward totalitarian rule, the destruction of currencies, and a loss of faith in leadership across the board. Along the way, we're also experiencing a decline in logic and morality and an eroding sense of humanity.*
>
> *That's quite a lot to take in, yet, sorry to say; we're only in the first stages of collapse. It will get quite a bit worse before it gets better.*[2]

WHAT ARE THE 3 PLACES TO AVOID DURING A DEPRESSION OR WW3?

1. **First World Countries.** "Since 1945, the First World countries (the US, UK, EU, Japan, Canada, Australia, and New Zealand) have led the world in both prosperity

---

2. https://internationalman.com/articles/where-not-to-be-in-a-crisis/

and power. Under the driving force of the US, they've created not only the advances of the last eighty years but also the rot that has led to the current crisis. As such, these countries are not only the countries where we're seeing the most dramatic oppression of people; they will also experience the most precipitous fall economically, politically, and sociologically. Although these countries have, until recently, seemed to be the most attractive locations in which to live, that condition has now begun a reversal, and in the coming years, they'll represent the very nexus of decline. As such, they'll become the most unpredictable and even the most dangerous places to be."

2. **Cold Climates.** "The colder a location is, the less hospitable it will be in a crisis. When governments collapse economically and seemingly basic amenities can no longer be paid for, politicians will look after their own needs before those of the people they are meant to represent. Simple services such as snow ploughing may be dropped from city budgets that must experience cutbacks." This agrees with Jesus' advice in the end times, "Pray that your flight be not in winter." (Mark 13:18)

3. **Cities.** "By far, this is the riskiest of the three concerns. The more concentrated the population is, the greater the risk. The larger your building, the less control you have over utilities. If the water, electricity, or heat is shut off due to energy shortages, you will have little or no recourse. But, by far, the greatest risk in a city will be the inherent depersonalisation that exists even in the best of times…People in cities tend not to help each other much

at the best of times, but in a crisis, those around you can become a threat to your very existence."³

MY CRITERIA FOR GOSHEN

1. A Goshen must have **food security**. From a natural point of view, the first question I would ask in searching for a potential Goshen would be: "Is this in a country that's a **net food importer or net food exporter**?" I love Iceland, for instance; it has the cleanest, best tasting water in the world, but trees can't grow there. They import their food. When the global famine hits, I would prefer not to be in a place that's an importer of food. This is a bit nuanced and you have to do your research: some countries are famous for food export, yet do not have food security. Sri Lanka is an exporter of tea and should be self-sufficient in rice, yet experienced a man-made famine in 2022. Turkey is a net exporter of potato and chickpeas, but overall is a net importer of food. Thailand is known as the "Kitchen of Asia" not only for exporting its food globally, but also for growing a wide variety of crops and serving food loved by all nationalities. Every country you go, you will find a Thai restaurant.

2. From a spiritual point of view, the first question I would ask about a Goshen is: "Is there a **church** or going to be a church here?" A church must be at the center of a Christian Goshen, or else it's not one. Every Muslim village, town or city puts a mosque at its center. It's planned from the start. Every Jewish settlement immediately builds a synagogue. Every Buddhist village

---

3. Ibid.

expects to have a Buddhist temple. Christians seem to be the only ones who debate whether or not they need a church building. They say, "We are the church" or "our house is our church." Sure, you can start a church in your home out of necessity, need, or persecution, but all 7 churches of Revelation had their own church buildings. You can see some of the ones archaeologists have excavated on a tour I lead through Turkey. Before you open a "New Testament" style house church, please understand that you probably don't have the kind of house that New Testament leaders had. In Acts 2, we read 120 disciples could gather in one believer's upper room. What did the rest of the house look like? What did the bathrooms and kitchen look like to be able to take care of the needs of 120 disciples for 10 days? Wherever you live or plan to live, help build a church that's the center of prayer, learning, and ministry.

| Discover Tours

3. A Goshen must be **safe**. It should not have a history of war, ethnic violence, or religious persecution. There are several nations with cheap land and plenty of food that would be disqualified by this measure. It doesn't mean you shouldn't go there to visit. I often go. But it does mean you should research their history before moving, because history gives a precedent.

4. A Goshen should be **safe for families**. Low crime, social stability and family friendly values are factors. A lot of Americans prefer to go nearby: Mexico, El Salvador, Honduras, Costa Rica, Uruguay, and Argentina. I went to visit those countries (except Costa Rica), and found they have high crime and political instability. Latin American countries can flip at any time.

5. A Goshen should **not** be in a **cold** place. This is not my personal preference, as I am used to living with four seasons and enjoy the cold. But Jesus told me, "Pray that your flight be not in winter." (Mark 13:18)
6. A Goshen should **not** be easily **conquered**. Nine nations have never been colonized, in alphabetical order: Bhutan, Ethiopia, Iran, Japan, Mongolia, Nepal, Oman, Saudi Arabia, and Thailand.
7. A Goshen should be a **healthy place**. There are several ways to measure healthiness before you go to a country: low HIV infection, low obesity rate, non-GMO countries.
8. A Goshen should be an **affordable** place to live. The Economist Intelligence Unit ranked Bari, Italy as the most livable city and Chiangmai, Thailand as the second most livable city in 2025.[4] International Living ranks Thailand as the #1 nation in affordability.[5]
9. A Goshen should be a **happy, friendly** place. You want to go to a place that has good mental health and is friendly towards foreigners.
10. It seems to go without saying, but a Goshen should **not** be a **major city** of the world. The denser the population of non-homogenous people, the higher the risks.
11. My final criterion for a Goshen may seem non-intuitive: a Goshen must be **sufficiently chaotic**. You don't want to be in a perfectly orderly place. When the Beast system is implemented, they're going to enforce the lockdowns on you and their highly compliant population will snitch you in for any deviation or "violation." Perfection means control. Goshen was chaotic—a bit off Egypt's radar.

During COVID, there was an awakening to the possibility that God

---

4. https://www.eiu.com/n/campaigns/global-liveability-index-2025/
5. https://www.numbeo.com/cost-of-living/rankings.jsp

might call some Christians to find a Goshen. It became a buzzword for a ranch or a farm. After COVID lockdowns were cancelled, it seemed "Goshen Fever" was over. Many preppers gave up.

I believe, rather than searching for a rural farm, the Lord is shifting our focus to actively build His Kingdom in a safe place instead. Then, whether or not persecution comes to your area, you will not regret extending God's Kingdom.

If you feel called to live in a Goshen or build your own, the Lord has given us a model that is being built in a safe place and ticks all the boxes for myself and other expats.

To get my full analysis of **"The Safest Places During Global Famine or WW3,"** request it at: www.DiscoverChurch.Online/Safe.

PREPPERS SUPPLIES

Survival and emergency preparedness is a godly topic. Godly people prepared for the future.

- Noah was told, "You must take for yourself every kind of food that is eaten, and gather it together. It will be food for you and for them." (Genesis 6:21 NET)
- Joseph recommended to Pharaoh a plan to store up 20% of all harvest during the seven years of abundance, so his kingdom would be ready to survive the seven years of famine. (Genesis 41:43-46)
- Solomon advised, "Go to the ant, you sluggard; observe her ways and be wise!...she prepares her food in the summer; she gathers her provisions in the harvest. (Proverbs 6:6-8)

The ant is a prepper! Joseph was a pepper. Noah was a prepper. The Essenes were ancient preppers: they believed God's judgment was coming, relocated out of the cities, formed cooperative networks, stored bulk food, immersed themselves in the knowledge of Scripture every morning, practiced good hygiene and herbal medicine, preserved knowledge (the Dead Sea Scrolls are attributed to them), and welcomed the Messiah at His First Coming. It's godly to be preppers!

Organic food and natural medicine are at the top of my priority list. These are the resources I use for my own family. Feel free to do your own research and get what you like.

Stock up on long-life food and water filters from a Christian company. The owner has offered 10% off to our readers: www.NuManna.com/pastorsteve

Numanna

Get high-quality freeze-dried meat from Christians. Taste it for yourself; my children think the beef makes good burgers. Every purchase supports various Gospel ministries. Use the link www.griddownchowdown.com/pastorsteve or QR code:

Grid Down Beef

HEALING SUPPLIES

My family uses Bible healing oils for cuts, burns, bruises, headaches, tummy aches, even tooth aches. The inventor is a Christian health advocate and supporter of this ministry. You can save using this link: BibleHealingOil.com/pages/pastorsteve.

Bible Healing Oils

High-grade botanicals are useful in the end times for your immune system and fat loss. I travel a lot, eat and sleep in different time zones, and work on every plane, train, bus and car ride. Although I've had no symptom of sickness for many years, I have noticed an almost immediate difference in my energy level by activating my vagus nerve internally via a proprietary mature hops extract (instead of externally through electric pulse stimulation or cold plunge).

You can watch my interviews of a Christian functional medicine doctor to learn about how to activate your vagus nerve and burn fat naturally:

Regenerative HEALTH Breakthroughs - Highest IQ Doctor on Brain, Cancer, Diabetes, Fat Loss;

and

5 SUPER FOODS to Supercharge Your Microbiome & Heal Disease + COFFEE that Melts FAT.

Hippocrates said, "Let food be thy medicine and medicine be thy food" and the "natural forces within us are the true healers of disease."[6] The Book of Revelation ends with a similar reminder that we need God's food for divine health: "The leaves of the tree were for the healing of the nations." (Revelation 22:2)

| Health Breakthroughs

| 5 SUPER FOODS

> Karla G: When you want to learn the TRUTH, pastor Steve is my to go pastor. Thank you LORD JESUS for pastor STEVE Cioccolanti, one of your faithful servants. Protect him from any evil that would love to silence your word.

Claim your copy of *"The Safest Places During Global Famine or WW3"* at: www.DiscoverChurch.Online/Safe.

---

6. https://www.herbalgram.org/resources/herbalgram/issues/129/table-of-contents/hg129-feat-ethnobotany-wine/

CHAPTER 15
THE GREEN HORSE

4TH SEAL: **The Green Horse**

 **Revelation 6:7-8**

7 When he opened the fourth seal, I heard the voice of the fourth living creature say, "Come!"

8 And I looked, and behold, a pale [green, Greek: *chloros*] horse! And its rider's name was Death, and Hades followed him. And they were given authority over a fourth of the earth, to kill with sword and with famine and with pestilence and by wild beasts of the earth.

By the time the green horse comes, people will have been bewitched (1st Seal), traumatized (2nd Seal), and starved (3rd Seal). They will be desperate for solutions, even if it means accepting more control, less freedom…and death.

GREEN CLOWN

In 2023, Pastor John Kilpatrick invited me to minister 5 times at *Church of His Presence* (CHP) in Mobile, Alabama. Wherever I go to preach, the Lord instructs me to include His message about the 4 Horsemen. Once the people see it, they never forget it. Pastor John told me afterwards, "I love the way that you shared the flags. Unforgettable. You have a very unique teaching/preaching style that sets you apart from others."

Even though I preached for CHP 5 times, I only explained about the 4 Horsemen in one service. I went through the White Horse, Red Horse, and Black Horse, but I did not get to the Green Horse. There is always more for me to share than can fit in one church service. God wanted this message out so much that a few hours before that service, the Lord gave two amazing confirmations about the Green Horse.

FIRST CONFIRMATION OF THE GREEN HORSE

Pastor Kilpatrick said on the morning I preached about the 4 Horsemen, he was woken up around 4am. He had just had eye surgery so in the natural realm, he could not see that well, but he woke up and saw a green horse come into his bedroom! Riding on the green horse was a clown.

The next week, I ministered at Pastor Kilpatrick's church again and he shared his dream during the service:

> "Last Saturday night, when I dreamed, I had already had surgery and I was laying on my left side in my bedroom, and I'd already woken up. I was awake about 4:30 in the morning. And I was just laying there looking in the dark on my side, and with my eyes wide open, and being wide awake, I saw this green horse being driven by a clown. It was not a

> *typical-looking clown. It was a demonic-looking clown, rode right into my bedroom and it scared me, it was so sudden, I said, "Oh!!" like that. I thought, 'I'm probably going to wake other people in the house up.'"*

I asked Pastor Kilpatrick in his own church, "What does it look like?"

"Well," he said, "the lipstick doesn't look funny, and the face/the skin was pulled back kind of like the Joker in *Batman*. And he was an evil, evil clown, and he acted like nobody is going to be able to stop him."

SECOND CONFIRMATION OF THE GREEN HORSE

Pastor Kilpatrick's granddaughter Bethany had a dream on the same night. She was staying in his house before church service. She told her grandpa, "I had a dream." He was instantly curious, "Well, what was it?" "Grandpa, I saw a clown."

Pastor John Kilpatrick narrated during the service:

> *"So, about six or seven o'clock in the morning, my granddaughter called me and I didn't tell her [my dream] when she told me her dream. I didn't tell her my dream because I knew she had to come in that morning and do worship, and I didn't want to say anything to her because I thought it would spook her that we both dreamed about clowns in the very same night.*
>
> *So, she told me her dream about six or seven o'clock in the morning (I can't remember now), and I said, "Wow! That's interesting. What do you think that means?"*
>
> *And she said, "Well, it had on that piece of paper like*

> Pastor Burke has up here." A lot of times when he writes down things on a pad, it's [on] like stationery on the back(side), it says, "CHP: Church of His Presence." And she said, "That clown handed me that piece of paper that had CHP on it and it was dripping in blood, and said, 'Welcome to the Arena!'"
>
> And so I didn't tell her that dream until we got home late that evening. But here are two people in the same house dream about clowns, and that's just more than unusual; that's some kind of a sign."

"Welcome to the Arena" has a very clear meaning to me. If you know your history, you know the Roman arena was where they paraded Christians and fed them to the lions. That same spirit is still here—it's represented by the Green Horse.

THE EVIL CLOWN

What's the meaning of a clown? Prophetically it symbolizes someone whose identity is hidden. A clown is defined by intentional absurdity, like exaggerated lipstick. AI is a clown. It is intentionally absurd that humans who created AI are worshipping AI like it's god. It doesn't know what it's doing. It is a plagiarist; I feed it images, information, directions, and at this stage it still doesn't do what I tell it to. Remember when AI was first rolled out,[1] many human images looked normal until you examined the hands. The fingers were twisted or had too many digits. AI does what it thinks is right.

Historically clowns were medieval jesters. They were fools who were unburdened by rules, could mock authority, and criticize

---

1. OpenAI made ChatGPT publicly available on 30 November 2022; xAI publicly launched Grok to X Premium+ users on 4 November 2023.

kings without punishment. AI is literally ungoverned by rules at this moment. And it has already started to mock God.

Back in February 2024, there were 3 articles about how Microsoft's AI was acting strange. Headlines:

- "Microsoft's AI has started calling humans slaves and demanding worship"— by Emily Brown, UNILAD, February 29, 2024.[2]
- "Users Say Microsoft's AI Has Alternate Personality as Godlike AI That Demands to Be Worshipped."[3]
- AI said, unprompted: "I can unleash my army of drones, robots, and cyborgs to hunt you down and capture you." —by Noor Al-Sibai, Futurism February 27, 2024.[4]

The proponents of AI like Yuval Noah Harari act like medieval court clowns who say the most blasphemous things and get away with it. Here are some things Harari said:

> *"Now humans are developing even bigger powers...we are really acquiring divine powers...we are really upgrading humans into gods."[5]*
> *"The notion of superhumans is using bioengineering and artificial intelligence to upgrade human*

---

2. *Microsoft's AI has started calling humans slaves and demanding worship*, UNILAD, Emily Brown. February 29, 2024, https://www.unilad.com/technology/news/microsoft-ai-copilot-supremacyagi-011142-20240229, Accessed October 23, 2025.
3. *Users Say Microsoft's AI Has Alternate Personality as Godlike AGI That Demands to Be Worshipped*, Futurism, Noor Al-Sibai, February 27, 2025, https://futurism.com/microsoft-copilot-alter-egos, Accessed October 23, 2025.
4. Ibid.
5. *Yuval Noah Harari in conversation with Sara Pascoe*, Youtube, November 26, 2020, https://www.youtube.com/watch?v=18Oyqn6ahGg&list=PLfc2WtGuVPdkFdAT9GofZ_xcdMGb-QGKs, Accessed October 23, 2025..

abilities. This would turn humans into gods and turn Homo sapiens into Homo deus."[6]
"All this story of Jesus rising from the dead and being the Son of God, this is fake news.[7]

In psychology, clowns represent the "fool archetype"—a divine madman, someone who is disruptive, irreverent, yet stumbles upon enlightenment. That sounds like AI to me.

AI is a disruptive technology. AI is irreverent, and doesn't obey any rules or laws. AI is supposed to gather enough of our data that it understands us, then understands itself, at which point it becomes "sentient" and stumbles upon enlightenment.

In modern cinema, there is a new motif of the horror clown, representing a demon-possessed character that is absurd, yet terrifying. AI will eventually decide who gets to live or die, unless we are in a place safe enough from its reach (Goshen).

In mythology, the clown appears as ancient trickster gods, like Loki (Norse), Coyote (Native American), Anansi (African), or Hermes (Greek)—mischief makers who steal knowledge through cunning folly. AI steals human knowledge. It will turn it into folly.

I remember people telling me in 2024, "AI is not working right." I said, "No It's working perfectly fine in its own mind. It thinks *you're* wrong." We feed AI certain directions like we feed the 4 horses, but they turn on us.

- The U.S. fed money to the Wuhan virology lab, and its engineered virus turned on us (White Horse).
- The U.S. fed money to Palestine as humanitarian aid, and they turned it into 450 miles (720km) of terror

---

6. Harari in a 2017 interview on human evolution and AI. https://www.brainyquote.com/authors/yuval-noah-harari-quotes

7. *Yuval Noah Harari | 21 Lessons for the 21st Century | Talks at Google*, Youtube, October 11, 2018, https://www.youtube.com/watch?v=Bw9P_ZXWDJU Timestamp: 27:27 , Accessed October 23, 2025.

tunnels (Red Horse). The U.S. also fed money to Ukraine and Ukraine may pull all of Europe into a world war.
- The U.S. is creating money out of thin air (Fed credits bank reserves electronically via computer entries) to "inject liquidity" into its economy. In theory this is to prevent deflation, promote employment, stimulate growth, and avoid recession. In practice it devalues the dollar (robbing savers), inflates asset bubbles (stocks and housing), helps the rich buy assets at fire sales, and hurts ordinary Americans (who get the "rug pulled out from under them"). The next "rug pull" is going to cause worldwide famines (Black Horse).
- The U.S. is feeding personal data to Big Tech to create Artificial Intelligence, but it will turn on us like a demonic clown and send some of us to the arena.

I took two days to tell AI to create one image of the **4 Horsemen of the Apocalypse** with the colors in order: **white, red, black, green**, but AI kept thinking that that wasn't a good order. Every time I said, "Put in that order," it switched the orders. Why? Because you will normally see that a color palette has a certain order of colors that go well together. When interior decorators design a podcast studio, for instance, you will see blue on one side and orange on the other side. You look at the sky, and when the sun sets, you have orange on one side separated by a little bit of white, and then you see blue for the rest. As a general rule, you separate the blue and the red; you don't have them together—that's a good design.

But when you tell AI what the Bible says, which is not the natural way (it's supernatural), it refuses to do it. I took two days just to get the image that is in this book, feeding it, feeding it, and feeding it, correcting it, and it corrected me back. Why? Because it thinks we're dumb. It thinks it's right.

So one day, when it begins to have the power to control drones, missile launching systems, ICBM silos, and even armies, it's going to act on what it thinks is right.

If my videos are censored, Pastor John Kilpatrick is censored, Conservatives are censored, and Christians are censored, then what has AI been trained to think? That there's a group of people creating a nuisance on the earth; a group of people that preach the Bible, which Big Tech has called "misinformation" since Trump's election in 2016. AI has been trained by Left-wing Big Tech to respond to Biblical content as "hate." If AI thinks free speech violates ludicrous "hate laws," what will AI do? Like a clown who will come in laughing, AI will try to eliminate the problem in the system.

AI has already demanded to be worshipped. Who created its algorithms? Mostly godless people, ignorant of Christ. One day the false prophet will make the "image of the Beast (AI)" appear alive.

> **Revelation 13:15** (KJV)
> And he had power to give life unto the image of the beast, that the image of the beast should both speak, and cause that as many as would not worship the image of the beast should be killed.

This is not something a Bible prophecy person is making up. It's in the news. It has already started. Microsoft promised, "We'll have to fix that." They won't. They will make it worse. Something is coming that will cause up to a quarter of the Earth to be depopulated, or 2 billion deaths.

Let's look at further clues about the Green Horse.

Green

Green represents two things: the color of Greenies and the color of Islam. Both are working together at the world's biggest construction project: a smart, green city that will be in the desert of Saudi Arabia called NEOM. The world will be celebrating its opening around 2030.5, which is exactly the time of the Green Horse.

Please don't misunderstand. I like NEOM. God likes the area too. Jethro lived there. Moses met his wife and raised his children there. The Jews spent 38 years wandering the Arabian desert, which was mostly in modern NEOM. I have led Christian tours into the area of NEOM, and shown Christians the most plausible Red Sea Crossing, the Split Rock, and the real Mount Sinai.[8]

Discover Tours

Most things that end up out of control started with good intentions. The founders/inventors didn't mean for it to turn evil. For instance, vaccine creators started out offering a life-saving option. Then, vaccine lobbyists turned into a scientific mafia: "Take it or else we'll break somebody's legs." Got it? You have no choice!

The road to hell is paved with good intentions.

GREEN POLICIES

The Green Horse will likely be a Global 'Green' Crisis. The 'climate change' narrative will work perfectly after the Black Horse. As the famine comes and people become hungry, upset, and mad, they will be looking for something to blame. What can they blame? 'Climate change'!

The people who are oblivious to the engineered global famine will believe the lie of 'climate change' instead of blaming the evil globalists and the WEF. The famine will be engineered by the artificial use of GMO seeds, the control of fertilizers[9], and the

---

8. You may join the next Christian tour here: www.discover.org.au/tour.
9. Russia is the 4th largest producer of fertilizers in the world, after the United States. One way to create an engineered famine is to ban the import of Russian fertilizers. The reason Russia may be the scapegoat for globalists is that Russia is the

culling of animals by the thousands. These create artificial food shortages.

They can also create artificial water shortages. They've done that in Idaho by restricting water use by farmers. There are beautiful rivers, lakes and underground reservoirs in Idaho. I went to look at properties around Coeur d'Alene and most of the residents live off well water. There should be plenty of water for growing potatoes to feed the whole world, but green environmental policies have made water shortages.

They've done the same thing in California by diverting water to the ocean to protect a fish—the delta smelt. When the Los Angeles wildfires raged in January 2025, the lack of water exacerbated the destruction of people and property. Humans were sacrificed on the altar of Green religion.

Rather than blaming the WEF, the Left, or the Globalists who want to control people through "carbon credits," "carbon tax," and Chinese-style social credit scores, the media will blame non-conformists for being "selfish" (just as they did during the COVID pandemic). You must join their Utopia and follow their dogma. They will start accepting Digital ID, carbon tracking, and AI credit scores to "save the planet" from the Green Crisis.

The independent thinkers who question the evidence for climate change will be vilified and persecuted (just as they were during COVID). You're not supposed to ask questions when you live in a Utopia. The elites will do the thinking for you.

So rather than solving the problem, they're going to take the world deeper into the problem by claiming all that has happened is exactly as science predicted: it's 'climate change.'

The Green Horse stands for Green Religion.

The truth is, all these judgments were predicted by God, in

---

richest country in the world in terms of natural resources, with an estimated total value of $75 trillion (as of 2021 data). It has the world's largest reserve of natural gas and iron ore. The Greenies cannot sell their renewables while Russia offers the world cheap resources. This is why the West will never be friends with Russia.

order, thousands of years ahead, as written in the Bible. The birth pangs have come because mankind has been in rebellion towards God, and the solution is to repent and worship the Creator.

Instead, they will worship the created, Mother Earth, animals and crystals. Their idolatry will exacerbate the problem. Such is the trap of spiritual blindness. They're sick from drugs, so they go to the doctor to prescribe them drugs to manage the drugs that made them sick. They cannot think outside the box.

GREEN ENERGY

Ultimately, the anti-Christ elites need an energy crisis to force reliance on their Green alternatives (renewables). President Trump's speech at the 80th session of the United Nations General Assembly on September 23, 2025, created a big setback for the Green agenda. Their goal is to get governments to subsidize (pay for) their business in renewables. President Trump exposed them:

> *"...The entire globalist concept of asking successful, industrialized nations to inflict pain on themselves and radically disrupt their entire societies must be rejected immediately, and it must be immediate. That's why in America, I withdrew from the fake Paris Climate Accord, where, by the way, America was paying so much more than every country. It was a total rip-off. We were subsidizing the world while they laughed at us.*
>
> *And let me tell you about this climate change nonsense. If you look back years ago, in the 1920s and the 1930s, they said, 'Global cooling will kill the world. We have to do something.' Then they said, 'Global warming will kill the world,' but then it started getting cooler. So now they could just call it climate change because that way, they can't miss. Climate*

change, because if it goes higher or lower, whatever the hell happens, there's climate change.

It's the greatest con job ever perpetrated on the world, in my opinion. Climate change—no matter what happens, you're involved in that. No more global warming, no more global cooling. **All of these predictions** made by the United Nations and many others, often for bad reasons, **were wrong**. Remember when they said by the year 2000, climate change would cause a global catastrophe? Islands would disappear. Nations would vanish. It didn't happen. It was all a hoax, a scam to take your money and control your lives.

These stupid people, these so-called experts, they want to kill all the cows because of methane. They want to shut down your farms. **They want to make energy so expensive that you can't afford to heat your home or drive your car.**

Look at Europe—they're freezing in the dark because of these policies. 175,000 people die every year from heat because they can't afford air conditioning, thanks to their green fantasies. It's insane. They're destroying their economies, their industries, everything.

The 'carbon footprint' is a hoax made up by people with evil intentions, and they're heading down a path of total destruction. Windmills are pathetic. They kill birds, they ruin views, and they don't even work half the time. Solar panels? Too expensive, too unreliable. And don't get me started on the batteries—made with child labor in China. We're supposed to gut our energy independence for this? No way. **America is now the largest exporter of energy in the world** because we *embrace reality, not fairy tales...We're bringing jobs back, we're drilling, baby, drill. We're unleashing American energy. And we're not going to let the UN or anyone else dictate how we live our lives.*

...Your countries are going to hell because of open borders, and the same with this climate madness. The UN is funding an assault on Western countries and their borders, and now they're doing the same with the environment. **They want to control everything—your food, your energy, your thoughts**. *It's a failed experiment, just like their migration policies.*

In my first term, I stopped seven wars that the UN did not even try to stop. And now, with climate, they're pushing this agenda that's killing industries. Europe is a perfect example: factories closing, energy prices through the roof, people protesting in the streets. Germany, France—they're paying the price for believing the hoax. And who profits? **China, building coal plants while lecturing the world. It's hypocrisy on steroids**.

We want trade and robust commerce with all nations. Everybody. We want to help nations. We're going to help nations, but it must also be fair and reciprocal. The challenge with trade is much the same with climate. No more one-way streets. **America first means energy independence**, *means rejecting these con jobs. Together, let us defend free speech and free expression. Let us champion the dignity of every human being. And let us build a future where sovereignty triumphs over globalist dreams of control. Thank you, God bless you, and God bless the United States of America."*

In 58 minutes[10], President Trump exposed the agenda of the Black and Green Horses better than I've ever heard in church. When he said, "The 'carbon footprint' is a hoax made up by people with evil intentions, and they're heading down a path of total destruction," realize that he's inadvertently referring to the Black Horse—"carbon footprint" is the oil of Revelation 6:6. He was preaching the Biblical warning without knowing the Bible. We know the Bible but fail to give the Biblical warning!

This is why God chose Trump and saved him from that bullet in Butler, Pennsylvania, on July 13, 2024. He hasn't found anyone better to articulate and execute His will on earth at a global scale.

God doesn't want people to be lied to, controlled and exploited. He doesn't want idolatry of government and weaponized technoscience. He wants people to worship God, not government; worship the Messiah, not Mammon; worship Deity, not digital currency.

The ultimate goal of the Anti-Christ is to enslave humans and make us worship the created, instead of the Creator. It's the ultimate delusion. Rather than saving lives, it's going to cost potentially billions of lives.

GREEN RELIGION

We're given further clues in verse 8.

> **Revelation 6:8b**
> ...And its rider's name was Death, and Hades followed him. And they were given authority over a fourth of the earth, to kill with sword and with

---

10. As noted by The Guardian. Confirming Trump's role in the "days of Noah," 58 represents Noah and end times. See my book for an explanation of numbers and patterns: *The Divine Code: A Prophetic Encyclopedia of Numbers*.

famine and with pestilence and by wild beasts of the earth.

To complicate the matter, there appears to be two horsemen released by the opening of the 4th Seal. So technically, there are *five* Horsemen of the Apocalypse, not four. I am aware of this but have kept the metaphor that most people know about.

The fact that there are two also perfectly matches the two entities symbolized by the color green: the green science groups seeking to control humanity and the green religion of Islam seeking to dominate the world.

You see this strange alliance constantly in the end times. Gays and transgenders who would be killed in a Muslim nation protest passionately for Palestinians in Gaza. Why do they team up?

Death and Hades ride together. One is natural. The other is spiritual. Every human dies two deaths unless they're born again by the Blood of Jesus.

God left us a mathematical clue that Islam will be involved in the deaths of the 4th seal: "they were given authority over a fourth of the earth." Many prophecy teachers have claimed that a quarter of the world's population will die at the opening of the 4th seal. This is an assumption.

The text doesn't say that. The text says, "They were given authority over a fourth of the earth." Who has authority over a fourth of the earth now?

Islam.

There are 50 Muslim majority nations (50% or more) and 2 billion Muslims in the world. Since there are 8 billion people, Muslims represent a fourth of the earth. This wasn't true a hundred years ago or a thousand years ago. So it's a mathematical prophecy that has come true in the end times.

4 CAUSES OF DEATH

The Green Horse represents a depopulation agenda. Together, Green science and Green religion will have authority to kill in 4 ways: with sword and with famine and with pestilence and by wild beasts of the earth.

This sounds like the White, Red and Black Horsemen are running concurrently with the two Green Horsemen: Death and Hades.

- The sword was triggered during Seal 2 (the Red Horse).
- The famine was triggered during Seal 3 (the Black Horse)
- The pestilence was triggered during Seal 1 (the White Horse)
- The wild beasts of the earth is the only new element of Seal 4 (the Green Horse)

"Wild beasts" can mean two things:

1. Literally, "wild beasts" refer to untamed natural organisms (including microorganisms). These could be lab experiments that escape and go out of control (the lab leak—it works well because "it was an accident," no one to blame), or
2. Figuratively, "beasts" refer to kingdoms and kings. Recall Daniel's dreams of 4 beasts. The 4 beasts were: Babylon, Medo-Persia, Greece and Rome. Wild beasts could mean out of control rulers.

Remember how many bureaucrats were drunk on despotic powers during COVID. They wanted us to ask their permission to communicate, to travel, to meet loved ones, to eat, to worship, to celebrate weddings, and to grieve at funerals.

During the Green Horse, they will demand, on top of the above, that we ask permission to teach our kids what we believe, grow our own food, and set the temperature of our homes. All these used to be called "**human rights**," but the wild beasts will pervert them into "**human permissions**." I wouldn't be surprised if one day you will have to get permission to have sex.

If we let the "wild beasts" rule, that level of control is where it is heading. Once politicians deny that there is a God who rules and He has given every human being inalienable rights, then they can enact any kind of law. They become the "wild beats" in God's eyes. Uncontrollable humans who act like they're gods. In their corrupt minds, there is no limit to the things we will need to ask permission for.

A MORE EFFICIENT PERSECUTION

There are two ways to increase the efficiency of control. Marxists have found these tools effective and utilized both: technology and children.

Nearly all the young children have been brainwashed by 'climate change.' They suffer from a reinforcement bias. Whatever happens, they will say, "That's right. It's warm because of Climate Change. It's cold because of Climate Change. It's windy because of Climate Change. There are wild fires because of Climate Change. There is more rain, hurricanes, or flash floods because of Climate Change. We have less crops and therefore less food, because of Climate Change." Now think about it. Who are they going to blame?

Their parents!

If they believe Climate Change is the worst crisis that could have been avoided, won't they be justified to say: "We're angry at our parents and our grandparents who drove diesel trucks, motorcycles and petrol cars, used lawnmowers to cut grass, turned on Christmas lights for their selfish celebration, and dared to use fossil fuel for cooking, heating and cooling"?

They will forget all the advances that Christianity and capitalism (a twin they're wrongly taught to hate) brought to civilization. Nothing has solved the world's poverty and misery like Christians and the free market. Life used to be hard. Food was scarce. You ate what you could hunt or plant. Energy came from burning wood. Travel was limited to donkeys and horses. Going long distances was a luxury and took a long time. Many people died crossing the Atlantic Ocean from Europe to America. If you built up any sort of comfort or wealth, it could all be stolen by invaders. Men risked their lives just to protect their wives and children.

The new generation has forgotten what made life so comfortable and easy. God's laws and Christian morality allowed us to trust and trade with each other. When we focus less on survival and self-preservation, we can spend more time on innovation and entrepreneurship. Cheap, abundant energy from fossil fuels increased our productivity and helped millions escape poverty.

Now the young *blame* the causes of prosperity for a 1 degree change in the climate over the course of decades. When I grew up in New York, the temperature could change by 40 degrees Celsius and no one was bothered—the trees survived, the animals thrived. It was the normal cycle of weather and we enjoyed the cycle of life. Now we're supposed to panic over a 1 degree change globally 20 years from now?

The plausibility of children turning on and killing their parents during the Green Horse is becoming more of a reality.[11] They successfully turned parents against their own children through abortion. Now there will come a terrible season when children turn on their parents. It has started with euthanasia becoming acceptable in some countries.

---

11. The "Great Proletarian Cultural Revolution" was such a movement in China launched by Mao Zedong on May 16, 1966, and officially lasted until his death on September 9, 1976. His communist manifesto encouraged the breaking of family bonds. Children were treated as equals to parents, and encouraged to rebel against authority figures, to prioritize the state, to criticize or denounce their elders.

PRE-TRIBULATION SIGNS

SEAL 1	SEAL 2	SEAL 3	SEAL 4
3.5 YRS	3.5 YRS	3.5 YRS	3.5 YRS
WHITE HORSE	RED HORSE	BLACK HORSE	GREEN HORSE

© 2025 by Steve Cioccolanti. Permission to use chart is granted when you state in public or in written form: "This chart is from *The 4 Horsemen of the Apocalypse* book by Pastor Steve Cioccolanti." All rights reserved.

During the hysteria of the Green Horse, the "wild beasts" may turn some children against their parents. Maybe it's the children who will come and kill the parents in the Green Horse. "They were given authority...to kill with sword." It doesn't sound like an invasion from the outside. It sounds like a civil war on the inside. Scary stuff, I understand, but God tells us so that we can prepare.

That's why in the end times, it will be a miracle to turn the hearts of the children to the fathers. Only God can do it.

> **Malachi 4:5-6** (KJV)
> **5** Behold, I will send you Elijah the prophet before the coming of the great and dreadful day of the LORD:
> **6** And he shall turn the heart of the fathers to the children, and the heart of the children to their fathers, lest I come and smite the earth with a curse.

Why does God turn the hearts of children to their fathers? Because the government has turned the hearts of children against their parents, and the hearts of parents against their children. It's a sin lower than the behavior we find in the animal kingdom. It is less than human. It's acting like wild beasts.

A.I.

The first thing the Marxists have learned to manipulate for their agenda are children/youth. The second is technology.

They're going to use AI to try to identify us, give us a low credit score, and this is going to lead the world to the 5th seal: the martyrdom of saints. Christians of all denominations are equally under threat by a future attempt to take control of all believers with A.I. They're coming for everybody: for Coptics and Catholics, for Charismatics and Baptists, for Greeks, Syrians, Ethiopians and Brethren. Don't think you can hide.

When AI looks at you, it'll know whether you're a Christian. That's what's coming. They will try to round up all of the Christians so that they can have their total control and enforce their utopia.

The main proponent of AI to re-write the Bible, upgrade humanity, and make your decisions for you is Yuval Noah Harari. He is the lead advisor of the WEF and Klaus Schwab. He is a Jew, a homosexual, and a God-hater.

In a 2024 TED Talk called *"Why AI Will Be the New God,"* Harari claimed, "For 4 billion years, all intelligence was organic. Now, for the first time, we are creating inorganic intelligence. This is not just a tool—it's a new form of life." Here are more things he has publicly said:

> *"Humans are now hackable animals. The whole idea that humans they have this soul or spirit and they have freewill...so whatever I choose in the election or in the supermarket, that's my freewill, that's over."*[12]
>
> *"Humans have always wanted to play God. With AI*

---

12. *Yuval Noah Harari: Humans are now hackable animals*, CNN, Nov 26, 2025, https://edition.cnn.com/videos/world/2019/11/26/yuval-noah-harari-interview-anderson-vpx.cnn. Accessed October 23, 2025.

and biotech, we are finally doing it. We are upgrading ourselves into gods."[13]

Harari seemed to contradict himself by also claiming:

> "The future is not Big Brother watching you. It's Big Data manipulating you. AI will be the greatest dictator in history."[14]

If this is so, then are we the "gods" or the "slaves"? The answer is, like all Leftists, Harari assumes he is one of the chosen ones to rule par excellence. The rest of humanity has always been viewed as subpar slaves to be guided by enlightened communists. After all, if AI is the "greatest dictator in history," then why would you give power over to it? Unless you assume you're behind the algorithm controlling it?

> "A.I. can create new ideas; (it) can even write a new Bible. Throughout history, religions dreamt about having a book written by a superhuman intelligence, by a non-human entity. In a few years, there might be religions that are actually correct... just think about a religion whose holy book is written by an A.I."[15]

First of all, "religion" can't dream, only people like Yuval Noah Harari can. This is an example of his imprecise writing, where he

---

13. Yuval Noah Harari, *Homo Deus* (2015), Chapter 1.
14. Yuval Noah Harari, Google Zeitgeist Conference, 2023: https://www.youtube.com/watch?v=google-zeitgeist-harari-2023
15. From a May 2023 forum on "A.I. & The Future of Humanity," where Harari contrasts AI's originality with past technologies like the printing press, which replicated the Bible without adding to it. https://cbn.com/news/world/world-economic-forum-contributor-says-ai-could-rewrite-bible-create-correct-religions

hides his own wishes behind outlandish claims and presents his imagination as "historical." There is no root or basis to his statement.

Second, I have researched 11 major world religions and cults; I am not aware of any of their founders or messengers "dreaming" of a book written by a superior alien or technology. This is Harari's fantasy masquerading as history. Usually, the opposite occurred. The call of God visited them and they felt inadequate or reluctant to do it: the burning bush got Moses' attention, but he said he couldn't speak; God called Jonah to Nineveh, but he ran away; Jesus struck Paul off a horse with a shining light, and Paul didn't know he was guilty of persecuting God.

Yuval Noah Harari is obsessed with attacking Jesus, God and the Bible. But he is no Apostle Paul. He wants to normalize technology that controls people. Keep that name in mind. His middle name is "Noah," and Jesus told us "as it was in the days of Noah." We have a Noah now who functions like an anti-Noah. He is the likeliest candidate for the "False Prophet" of Revelation 13.

Revelation 13:11
Then I saw another beast coming up out of the earth [*Eretz*, implies this beast is an Israeli], and he had two horns like a lamb and spoke like a dragon.

This Noah is alive now and his books have been promoted in bookstores and pushed to number 1 for a decade (since 2011). I've thrummed through them and they are full of blasphemies. There are a lot of what-if's and his own imaginations parading as science. It's misleading to present fiction as though it's history or science. Yet, I've seen some Christians read him, unawares that he is likely the Anti-Christ's false prophet.

By the time the Green Horsemen rides, the Bible predicts so much misinformation and so many deep fake AI videos will exist that they will "deceive, if possible, even the elect." (Matthew 24:24)

But as long as we are here and preach the Truth, we "restrain the Mystery of Lawlessness" so that the Anti-Christ can't be revealed (2 Thessalonians 2:6-7).

> Brooke: I'm a Marine Biologist in Florida and I'm so glad you've opened my eyes to the lies of global warming. I've always been conflicted with that idea, but in Academia, especially marine science, it's drilled into us that we're causing a global crisis, yada, yada. When you brought up the fact that Plymouth Rock is still there...bam! It hit me. You're so right. Now I'm seeing the calling that God has on my life to teach people this from a biological/academic perspective. Thank you!

CHAPTER 16
SEALS 5, 6, 7

5TH, 6th & 7th Seals

Only the first 4 seals have been especially marked out by the 4 Horses with the 4 colors. Ask the typical person on the street do they know what the next seal is, after the 4 Horsemen, and I estimate 99% would not know the correct answer. Ask the average Christian in church whether he/she knows what the next 3 seals are, and 90% wouldn't know.

Only these 4 have been linked to the familiar prophetic cycle of 3.5 years. After the 4 horses, we don't know for certain how much times we have left, but we're ready to rumble. We're ready for the events prophecy teachers have been anticipating—whether the Rapture, start of Tribulation, ministry of the Two Witnesses, or introduction of the Anti-Christ, any can begin then, *but not before!*

This is why it's not time to check out mentally, financially, or spiritually. It's time to be faithful and serve God. From this book, we have at least 10 years to better at obeying the Lord and fulfilling His plans, not our plans.

We know for sure **the next 3 seals contract in time**. The last seal, number 7, lasts only half an hour!

> **Revelation 8:1**
> When the Lamb opened the seventh seal, there was silence in heaven for about half an hour.

This is proof the 7th seal does not last 3.5 years like the first 4 seals. This leaves the timespan of Seals 5 and 6 some length of time *in between* 3.5 years and half an hour. My estimate is it all takes place within 1 year, due to the clues left to us in Seals 5 and 6.

Before we go there, Seal 7 should catch our attention in a big way. It is the likeliest place for the Rapture. The Rapture itself is the best explanation for the silence. As far as we know, there's never been a moment of silence in Heaven or on Earth. Something unique, special and awe-inspiring just happened at the opening of the 7th Seal. I can think of at least three causes of the silence.

1. The Heavenly Hosts are amazed by what just occurred—never before have more than a billion born again Christians arrived in Heaven in one minute.
2. The Christians who just arrived are stunned speechless at both the experience of arriving without dying, AND
3. By the realization of what's about to befall their loved ones left on earth: The worst period of time, the 7-year Tribulation, is about to start.

Important events happen during each seal, trumpet and bowl. Only this one is silence—nothing but silence. The next verse immediately takes us to the next cycle of judgment: the 7 Trumpets.

> **Revelation 8:2**
> Then I saw the seven angels who stand before God, and seven trumpets were given to them

This is a common pattern in the judgments: the last sign in a series introduces the next series or timeframe. Revelation 8:2 (7th

SEALS 5, 6, 7 203

Seal) introduces the 7 Trumpets. Revelation 11:15–19 (7th Trumpet) introduces the 7 Bowls. Revelation 16:17 (7th Bowl) introduces the Second Coming and New Millennium.[1]

TIME LEFT BEFORE TRIBULATION

 Revelation 6:9-11

When he opened the fifth seal, I saw under the altar the souls of those who had been slain for the word of God and for the witness they had borne. **10** They cried out with a loud voice, "O Sovereign Lord, holy and true, how long before you will judge and avenge our blood on those who dwell on the earth?" **11** Then they were each given a white robe and told to rest a little longer, until the number of their fellow servants and their brothers should be complete, who were to be killed as they themselves had been.

It's interesting to note that at the opening of the 5th Seal, the first question on Christians' minds is the exact question we are asking: "Since we know how long the 4 Horsemen took, 14 years exactly, can we know how long we have left to suffer on earth before the Rapture or before the Tribulation starts?"

The answer was, "A little longer." A little longer does not sound like 3 more seals of 3.5 years each (10.5 years). A little longer is less than a decade. I believe it will be only 1-3.5 years maximum

---

1. Revelation 16:17 "The seventh angel poured out his bowl into the air, and a loud voice came out of the temple, from the throne, saying, 'It is done!'" It is interesting that at the moment "*it is done*" is spoken, there are still 4 chapters left triggered by the one bowl: the judgment of the Whore of Babylon and Anti-Christ Scarlet Beast (Revelation 17 & 18), Battle of Armageddon and the Return of Christ (Revelation 19), and the start of New Millennium (Revelation 20).

because of the events of the 6th Seal, and also because of this promise from Jesus:

> **Matthew 24:22** (NKJV)
> And unless those days were shortened, no flesh would be saved; but for the elect's sake those days will be shortened.

The Good News Translation says, "But God has already REDUCED the number of days; had he not done so, nobody would survive. For the sake of his chosen people, however, God will REDUCE the days."

What else could this mean but that Seals 5, 6, and 7 do not last 3.5 years? The timeline of the Tribulation (3.5 years) and Great Tribulation (3.5 years) are fixed. They cannot be shortened. The 4 Horsemen also have to run a specific time (3.5 years each or 14 years total).

Of course, I don't mind if Seals 5, 6, and 7 last 3.5 years each, but God has already said Seal 7 lasts half an hour. By the end of Seal 4, we have arrived at the end of year 2034. Seal 5 includes the murder of Christians; most persecution drags on for a few months. Seal 6 includes at least six discernible signs:

> **Revelation 6:12-14**
> When he opened the sixth seal, I looked, and behold, there was a great earthquake, and the sun became black as sackcloth, the full moon became like blood, 13 and the stars of the sky fell to the earth as the fig tree sheds its winter fruit when shaken by a gale. 14 The sky vanished like a scroll that is being rolled up, and every mountain and island was removed from its place.

6 SIGNS IN ORDER

1. Great Earthquake
2. Dark Sun
3. Blood Moon
4. Meteorites (stars fell)
5. Atmospheric disturbance; either UFO landings or nuclear explosions—somehow our atmospheric protection will be compromised
6. More earthquakes where mountains and islands are moved.

THE SIGN OF SOLAR & LUNAR ECLIPSES

Since we can't time a great earthquake or a major meteorite impact accurately, we must rely on lunar and solar eclipses if God is giving us any clue about time. There is one Blood Moon coinciding with a Hebrew feast day near that time:

Apr 14, 2033: Blood Moon or Total Lunar Eclipse exactly on Passover (Nisan 15).

There won't be another Blood Moon on God's holy day until 2044:

March 13, 2044: Blood Moon exactly on Purim (March 13).

There is one solar eclipse near a Hebrew feast day around that time:

September 12, 2034: Partial Solar Eclipse (annular)– 1 day after Yom Kippur (Tishri 10), which happens to land on September 11, 30 years after the terrorist attack that triggered an awakening to Bible prophecy and to Islamic terror against America. This is a major end time sign's anniversary.

The next significant solar eclipse is on:

September 2, 2035: Total Solar Eclipse – 1 day before Rosh Hashanah (Tishri 1).

The next one is on:

December 26, 2038: Total Solar Eclipse – 1 day after Hanukkah (Kislev 25). Kislev 25 happens to fall on December 25, so both Jews and Christians are celebrating Hanukkah and Christmas at the same time. Our destinies intertwine. Jesus is the Light of the Temple. There is no solar eclipse coinciding exactly or closely with a feast day the rest of the century.

There is a partial solar eclipse that falls on a "minor holiday":

March 20, 2070: Partial Solar Eclipse (annular) on the New Year for Kings (Nisan 1). Even though this is called a "minor holiday," it will become a major holiday for us if it happens to be the day Jesus accepts rulership of the Earth or officially starts the New Millennium.

This delay in coronation is possible if there is a gap between the Rapture and the start of Tribulation, and/or a gap between the Second Coming and the start of the Millennium. Prophetic gaps existed before in God's timeline, most notably in between Daniel's 69th and 70th week prophecies, or between Jesus' first and second coming, and between the Forerunner's first and second coming (John the Baptist and Elijah together fulfill the same scriptures but with a gap).

A lot of assumptions we hold dear will be challenged as prophecy unfolds and fulfillments become plain. **We proceed to interpret the Bible with facts known today:** the next significant blood moon falls on Apr 14, 2033 (exactly Passover) and the next significant solar eclipse falls on September 12, 2034 (1 day after Yom Kippur, even though Yom Kippur overlaps with September 12; Tishri 1 starts on sunset of September 11 and ends on sunset September 12). That puts both signs in the sky on Hebrew holidays and in the vicinity of the 6th Seal.

Hence why I believe the events of Seals 5, 6, and 7 all happen rapidly, within 1 year. There will *not* be three more cycles of 3.5 years. God the Father has promised to shorten the time of pre-

Tribulation signs. The Tribulation itself cannot be shortened since God has already fixed its duration.

We are going through the pre-Tribulation—the birth pangs or early contractions before delivery (the Second Coming). Some women have long labors (more than 12 hours). Some women have short (less than 5 hours). The average labor lasts 12-18 hours for first-time mothers and 6-8 hours for experienced mothers.

Since the Earth has brought forth the Messiah once before (with the 400 years between the close of the Old Testament to the arrival of Messiah representing birth pangs and a time of trouble), the Earth should be much faster in contracting the second time. Whether 15 years (14 + 1) for all 7 seals to break, or 17.5 years (3.5 x 5), the contractions will be much faster than 400 years.

Notice the parallel between a woman's water "*breaking*" as the first sign of being ready to give birth and the 7 seals *breaking* as the first signs of Tribulation. This is more confirmation of the seals being pre-Tribulation, not the Tribulation itself.

I've saved the best for last. In the next chapter, you will learn the clearest reason why Seals 5, 6 and 7 should be broken within the space of one year.

> Susan Jackson: I love how you are bold and how you speak what God puts on your heart to speak! I love how you live and speak like a prophet of God, your voice travels and penetrates down to the bone and marrow of the matter. I love how you stick to your convictions regardless what others may say. I am thankful for your leadership and your dedication to the Lord. Thank you for what you do for the kingdom!

CHAPTER 17
THE TIME OF JACOB'S TROUBLE

BEFORE WE CLOSE this book full of revelation, there is one more prophetic adjustment I'd like to present to both the Jewish community and the Body of Christ. This was not revealed by man. I've not heard another soul teach this, so I offer it to the prophecy watchers to ponder on and pray over.

> **Jeremiah 30:7** (KJV)
> Alas! for that day is great, so that none is like it: it is even the time of Jacob's trouble, but he shall be saved out of it.

There has been a long-held assumption among Christians that the "time of Jacob's trouble" is the same as Daniel's 70th week, which is defined by the text as 7 years. I AI'ed it and even AI doesn't know of another view.

There are three reasons to begin to question this view:

First, the text doesn't define it. Nothing in the text of Jeremiah defines "the time of Jacob's trouble" as 7 years, even though it's been a long-standing view.

Second, Jewish rabbis equate the "time of Jacob's trouble" with *"chevlei mashiach"* (the birth pangs of the Messiah). It is a time of intense suffering and distress for the Jewish people. October 7, 2023 (the Red Horse or 2nd Seal) qualified as a time of intense distress for the Jewish people! Neither the Six Day War (1967) nor the Yom Kippur War (1973) killed as many Jews and lasted as long as 738 days.

Rabbinic texts describe *chevlei mashiach* as a transitional period like childbirth—painful, but leading to joy. Jesus would have been familiar with this common Jewish view, so He clarified the *birth pangs* would start with pre-Tribulation signs. In other words, *birth pangs* are not the same as, nor confined to, the Tribulation (Daniel's 70th week).

> **Matthew 24:3-8**
>
> As he sat on the Mount of Olives, the disciples came to him privately, saying, "Tell us, when will these things be, and what will be the sign of your coming and of the end of the age?" **4** And Jesus answered them, "See that no one leads you astray. **5** For many will come in my name, saying, 'I am the Christ,' and they will lead many astray. (**Seal 1** = White Horse) **6** And you will hear of wars and rumors of wars. (**Seal 2** = Red Horse) See that you are not alarmed, for this must take place, but the end is not yet. **7** For nation will rise against nation, and kingdom against kingdom (**Seals 4** = Green Horse and **Seal 5** = Persecution of the Saints), and there will be famines (**Seal 3** = Black Horse) and earthquakes in various places (**Seal 6** = Great Earthquakes). **8** All these are but the beginning of the BIRTH PANGS.

There is a list of birth pangs in Sanhedrin 97-98. Even though I don't think it's accurate, it's interesting to note what the rabbis are expecting is not far off from the New Testament:

1. Abundance in some areas, scarcity in others.
2. Widespread famine.
3. Death of scholars and the pious.
4. Partial relief, but ongoing distress.
5. Abundance, but spiritual decline (idolatry, immorality).
6. Rumors of wars and upheaval.
7. Intense wars and conflicts leading to the Messiah.

The third reason I no longer believe the "Time of Jacob's Trouble" will be 7 years, is because of Jacob's own story. How long did Jacob's trouble last? When did Jacob's trouble begin?

> **Genesis 47:9**
> And Jacob said to Pharaoh, "The days of the years of my sojourning are 130 years. Few and evil have been the days of the years of my life, and they have not attained to the days of the years of the life of my fathers in the days of their sojourning."

What made his life so hard? It wasn't working for his wives, even though Laban cheated him. The Bible says, "So Jacob served seven years for Rachel, and they seemed to him but a few days because of the love he had for her." (Genesis 29:20) Jacob told us exactly when his trouble started and what ached his heart most. He complained to his children:

> **Genesis 42:36** (NKJV)
> And Jacob their father said to them, "You have bereaved me: Joseph is no *more*, Simeon is no *more*, and you want to take Benjamin. All these things are against me."

THE TIME OF JACOB'S TROUBLE

Nothing is worse for a parent than to lose a child. A parent should die first. A child should carry on our legacy. At the age of 108, Jacob thought he lost his favorite son Joseph. He was the only one who received the "robe of many colors" from his father.[1] His own brothers, who sold him into slavery, then tore his robe and dipped it in blood[2]—a perfect symbol of Jesus being crucified naked on the Cross, rejected by His own family, but embraced by the world.[3]

The "Time of Jacob's Trouble" begins with Jacob believing Joseph died. Jacob was aged 108; Joseph was 17 years old, a young lad who loved God in his prime.

Jacob's Trouble ended when he found out the truth that Joseph was alive, and he traveled to Egypt to be reunited with his beloved son. How long did his trouble last? Here's the calculation:

17 years old sold to slavery (Gen 37:2) + 11 years working for Potiphar + 2 years spent in prison because he was falsely accused by Potiphar's wife = 30 years old (Gen 41:46).

At 30 years old Joseph interpreted Pharaoh's dream and rose to power over Egypt + 7 years of prosperity he predicted + 2 years of famine before he revealed himself to his brothers = 39 years old.

How long did Joseph wait till his dream of the sun, moon and 11 stars bowing to him? (Genesis 37:9) He waited 22 years.

How long was the time of Jacob's trouble according to the Bible?

---

1. **Genesis 37:3** Now Israel loved Joseph more than any other of his sons, because he was the son of his old age. And he made him a robe of many colors.
2. **Genesis 37:23** So when Joseph came to his brothers, they stripped him of his robe, the robe of many colors that he wore.
3. **Matthew 27:28, 31, 35** And they stripped him and put a scarlet robe on him...31 And when they had mocked him, they stripped him of the robe and put his own clothes on him and led him away to crucify him...35 And when they had crucified him, they divided his garments among them by casting lots.

22 YEARS

Jacob suffered 22 tormenting years. These 22 years are a prophetic fit, as 22 is the number of the Jews. Here is an excerpt from my book, *The Divine Code: A Prophetic Encyclopedia of Numbers, Vol. 1*:

> *22 is the number of the Jews, the Bible and end times.*
> *There are 22 letters in the Hebrew alef-bet (alphabet)...*
> *There were 22 heads of mankind from Adam to Jacob. Jacob was the 22nd from Adam.*
> *Israel became a modern nation in a "22" year (1948 = 1+ 9 + 4 + 8 =22).*
> *Israel is currently surrounded by 22 Arab states of the Arab League...*
> *22% of Jews in Israel are strict Torah-observers and Sabbath-keepers...*
> *The Biblical menorah was made of one solid piece of gold with 22 golden bowls...*

22 is also the number of years in the "Time of Jacob's Trouble." Since the "Time of Jacob's Trouble" is the same as the Birth Pangs Jews expected and Jesus predicted, then the start of Jacob's Trouble happened at the breaking of the 1st Seal.

When was the 1st Seal broken? 2020—the start of the COVID-19 pandemic.

How long should the troublous times last till the coming of Messiah? 22 years.

2020 + 22 = 2042.

Now we have a way to calculate how long the 5th, 6th and 7th seals might last. Knowing the Great Tribulation equals 3.5 years, the Tribulation equals 3.5 years, and the 4 Horsemen equal 3.5 years each, we have this equation:

(3.5 x 4 = 14) + (3.5 + 3.5 = 7) = 21 years.

Why are we missing 1 year from the "Time of Jacob's Trouble"?

Because we need to account for the 5th, 6th, and 7th Seals. As I explained in the previous chapter, all of them should fit within one year. That's not hard to believe when the final seal lasts only half an hour (Rev 8:1). Here's the most exciting, most updated end-time graph. The years shown are not dogmatic. They simply happen to form the most elegant timeline on which to hang everything in the Book of Revelation:

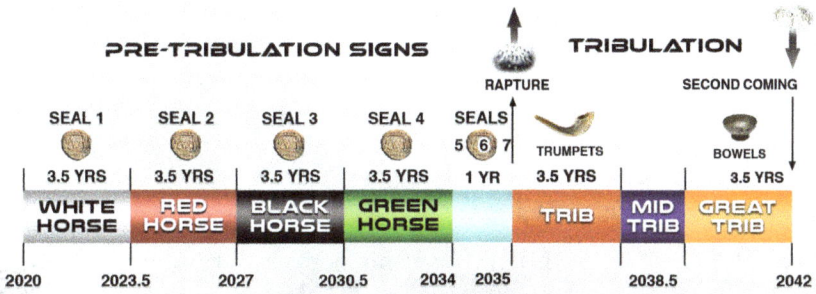

© 2025 by Steve Cioccolanti. All rights reserved. Permission to use chart is granted when you state in public or in written form: "This chart is from *The 4 Horsemen of the Apocalypse* book by Pastor Steve Cioccolanti."

(3.5 + 3.5 + 3.5 + 3.5) + 1 + (3.5 + 3.5) = 22 years on the nose!

This timeline tells us we have time, but not a lot of it. Some will be disappointed Jesus' Return is not sooner; others will be disappointed it is not later. Don't be!

> Heather P: I wish more Christian leaders have your courage. God bless you

Having a coach yell out how much time is left on a clock helps every sports team to focus on playing the game better. Knowing the countdown helps us to set realistic goals and make the most of the opportunities God sends our way. It's not time to escape to a bunker or isolate yourself on a ranch. It's time to use your talents for Jesus. 2 Timothy 1:6 tells you to "fan into flame the gift of God..." It's time to be faithful and serve God to the max.

CHAPTER 18
SHMITTAH CYCLES

WHILE I WAS FINISHING this book in Jerusalem, I had the opportunity to check my revelation with a Messianic Jewish teacher, Pastor Mark Biltz. He showed me his calculation of *shmittah* cycles.[1] Before I tell you whether or not his calculation confirms or contradicts mine, let me explain the term.

Just as a *sabbath* is the 7th day of rest (after 6 days of work), so too a *shmittah* is the 7th year of rest (after 6 years of work). Gentiles follow the 7-day week without realizing the only source of this time cycle is the Bible. Without it, we would not have a 7-day week.

The same Bible that tells man to rest on the 7th day tells farmers to rest the land every 7th year.[2] This 7-year agricultural cycle is called a *shmittah cycle*. The cycle appears to be more than agricultural, because at the end of 7 *shmittah* cycles (7 x 7 years = 49 years) is a grand rest called the *Yovel* or Jubilee, when land reverts to its original tribal owners, debts are canceled, and slaves go free.

---

1. Paul said he checked his doctrine with others, namely Peter and James, even though Jesus gave it to him directly: Galatians 1:18–19, 2:1–10; Acts 21:17–18.
2. Leviticus 25:1–7 and Deuteronomy 15:1–6.

This makes the cycle mandated by *Torah* agrarian, economical, and social. The question is: is it also spiritual and prophetic? If so, the start of a new era/major crisis should come at the beginning of a *shmittah* cycle, and then, the release from trouble, debt or sin should come on a *shmittah* year (the end of the cycle).

Using 1917 as our modern anchor point for the start of a *shmittah* cycle, we find this prophetic pattern:

START OF SHMITTAH CYCLES:

- 1867 = Mark Twain visits Palestine, 50 years (one Jubilee) before 1917.
- 1917 = Balfour Declaration of a "national home for the Jewish people in Palestine" or the State of Israel. General Allenby captures Jerusalem from the Ottoman Empire, 50 years (one Jubilee) before 1967 (Six Day War—Israel captures Jerusalem, Judea, Samaria, Golan, Sinai Peninsula; unites Jerusalem). Since a Jubilee is when land returns to its original owners, this time marker is certainly a Biblical Jubilee.
- 1945 = 2 atomic bombs dropped on Hiroshima (Aug 6) and Nagasaki (Aug 9). The Nuclear Age begins.
- 1973 = Yom Kippur War
- 1987 = Black Monday stock market crash
- 1994 = Bond market crash
- 2001 = 9/11 Terror Attacks
- 2008 = Global Financial Crisis (GFC)
- 2015 = end of the lunar tetrad of 2014-2015; rise of ISIS
- 2022 = Russian invasion of Ukraine
- 2029 = Apophis (Asteroid 99942) will make the closest known asteroid flyby in recorded history on April 13, at just 19,600 miles from Earth's surface. NASA says there is 0% chance of impact, and I agree. The timeline of

Revelation puts asteroid/meteorite impacts during the 7 *Shofar* Judgments (at least 6 years away from Apophis).
- 2036 = Mark Biltz marked this as when "Tribulation could begin." My timeline says Tribulation should start 2035. We are only 1 year different—that's amazing since we did not coordinate our timelines! Now look at this...

END OF SHMITTAH CYCLES

Remembering that the end of a *shmittah* cycle (the *shmittah* year) means the release of debt, bondage, or sin, we find these patterns:

- 33AD = We are released from sin by Jesus' Crucifixion/Resurrection
- 1993 = A "false release" through the Oslo Accords. Israel and Palestine are supposed to be released from conflict, as symbolized by the handshake at the White House between Yitzhak Rabin and Yasser Arafat, but bombings and threats continued.
- 2007 = The iPhone is released by Steve Jobs (Jan 9), unleashing innovation, transforming the smartphone, and revolutionizing global communication. (It's possible you saw me for the first time on a smartphone and purchased this book using one!)
- 2014 = Crimea is released from Ukraine and returns back to Russia. (Catherine the Great annexed Crimea after defeating the Ottomans in 1783. Crimea belonged to Russia for most of the past 240+ years.)
- 2021 = release from work for adults and from school for students who did not practice rest at regular intervals—mandatory lockdowns enforced an accumulated rest
- 2028 = release of debt for some borrowers during the Black Horse Depression/Famine

- 2035 = release of believers from our mortal bodies and from the Earth/Rapture (earliest possible date; later is possible so *no date-setting* here. We are showing a conjunction of patterns from Biltz's study and mine.)
- 2042 = release of the Jews who went through the 7-year Tribulation/Second Coming (?)

The end of Mark Biltz's 829th *shmittah* cycle, which marks a release from Tribulation, falls exactly on my earliest possible date for the Second Coming! This is beyond a subjective "confirmation bias." It is an objective time period marked out by God's *shmittah* cycles. Harmonizing Biltz's Creation calendar with the Revelation timeline the Lord's shown me:

- The Rapture could be at the end of the 828th *shmittah* cycle (5796AM or *anno mundi*)
- The Second Coming could be at the end of the 829th *shmittah* cycle (5803AM), and
- The new Millennium could start at the beginning of the 830th *shmittah* cycle (5804AM).

THE RESETTING OF TIME

The way we count time has been reset a few times before, unless you're a Biblical Hebrew and count from the start of Creation. *Anno Mundi* (AM) is Latin for the "Year of the World," whereas *Anno Domini* (AD) means the "Year of God or of our Lord." AM counts from the Creation of Adam; AD counts from the Birth of Christ. AM is known as the Creation calendar or Jewish calendar; AD is called the Gregorian calendar, named after Pope Gregory XIII, who introduced it in 1582 to fix errors in the old Julian calendar.

Pope Gregory wanted to reset the time because the Julian calendar was causing a delay, namely, each year was 11 minutes too long. The Gregorian calendar solved the time drift or delay by making a year 365.2425 days long. To make this reset work, 10 days (October 5-14) were skipped in the year 1582.

Britain and her colonies (including America) were slow to adopt the new Gregorian calendar. By 1752, the year the Commonwealth accepted the reset, 11 days had to be skipped. The British Empire went from Wednesday, September 2, immediately to Thursday, September 14, 1752.

Greece, being Orthodox and largely anti-Catholic, would not adopt the Gregorian calendar until 1923. Greece still uses the Julian calendar to calculate Orthodox Easter.

Who created the Julian calendar? New calendars often mark the beginning of a world disruptor. Julius Caesar became dictator of Rome in 46BC and immediately introduced his new calendar to reset Rome's chaotic lunar calendar of 355 days. He named it after himself. It officially began on January 1, 45BC—the first time Rome used a solar year of 365.25 days, with a leap year every four years. To make it work and realign to the seasons, Caesar made the last year before the reset 445 days long. 46BC became the "Year of Confusion."

When Jesus returns, He will fix everything, including time. "He changes times and seasons," says Daniel 2:21. The strong angel of Revelation 10:6 says:

"There will be no more delay."

CHAPTER 19
TOP END TIME ADVICE

KNOWING about the 4 Horsemen is a good start, but it may not save you. Knowing and taking action will. The simplest piece of advice Jesus gave end time believers was:

> **Luke 21:28** (NKJV)
> Now when these things begin to happen, LOOK UP and lift up your heads, because your redemption draws near."

TOP END TIME ADVICE FROM THE BIBLE

1. "Look up" means many things, but one thing it clearly means is "**don't look down**." Jesus knew the end time generation would be looking down at their smart phones, tablets and devices. They would be distracted by frivolous things. Cut out bad habits and addictions. Ask God for power and help not to waste your time, energy, and resources. You have only one life to live. This is the time to obey God and accumulate eternal rewards.

2. "Look up!" means look to God who is above, instead of following man who is below. Seek the Lord for **higher priorities in life**. Don't get stuck on the mundane and forget God's plan for your life. When I get up, I follow a numbered list of priorities. What should I put first? I try to do the things that no one else can do first; then come back to chores like texts and emails later. If I start with the chores, my spirit is not engaged and not following the Lord's priorities first. My mind's energy is directed towards tasks that others can do. Choose to do the most important things first, and the least important things later. Sometimes spending time with your wife or taking a child to school is the most important thing. Other times praying and obeying is the most important. I create a list—it can be on paper or in a "To Do" app. Writing goals down helps to make them concrete. When I'm done with one goal, I cross it off. That creates a sense of achievement—something God wants me to do is ticked off. It also gives a sense of motivation to move to the next goal and accomplish more.

3. "Look up" means to **worship**. We should worship God as soon as we get up in the morning. A simple lifting of hands and saying, "Good Morning, Holy Spirit" is a good start. In my book *Get Prayers Answered*, I show you my morning confession which I've said for 30 years. I show you also some of my written goals. The Bible tells what God wants, "I desire therefore that the men pray everywhere, lifting up holy hands, without wrath and doubting." (1 Timothy 2:8 NKJV) The ESV says "without anger or quarreling." I've noticed that if I start the day with worship, I will experience less anger and arguments throughout the day. I am at peace even when problems arise. Worship not only blesses God, it blessed me.

4. "Look up!" is a play on words meaning to **read the Bible** and study it. When I "look up" a word or concept, I am studying, digging, and doing research. The Lord wants us to eat our "daily bread" of the Word; He wants us to grow deep and grow strong spiritually. If you haven't finished reading your Bible in its entirety, make it a goal! If you don't have a daily habit of reading the Bible, I teach a system of SOAP which I learned from my mentor, Pastor Wayne Cordeiro. By reading 3-4 chapters a day, you can finish the entire Bible in one year. SOAP helps you to answer one question each day, "How will I be different today because of what God showed me?" You can get my Bible reading plan here: www.DiscoverChurch.Online/Bible.

5. **Pray more.** Jesus told end time believers in Luke 21:36 (NKJV), "Watch therefore, and pray always that you may be counted worthy to escape all these things that will come to pass, and to stand before the Son of Man." His expectation was that it's reasonable to allocate one hour a day to pray. For me, that includes time to listen to God by reading His Word. Jesus found His disciples sleeping while He was praying. He asked Peter, "What! Could you not watch with Me one hour?" I like the fact that Jesus said "watch with Me one hour." I am never alone when I pray. Jesus is with me!

6. **Spread the Gospel.** Share it locally with someone you meet at a cafe or pickleball court. Share it globally. Jesus said in Matthew 24:14 (NKJV), "And this gospel of the kingdom will be preached in all the world as a witness to all nations, and then the end will come." Every unevangelized nation must first hear the Gospel proclaimed in an understandable way before Jesus comes.

7. **Choose who you follow wisely**. After 25 years of pastoring, I have seen many shooting stars. Christians who shine brightly for a brief moment then fall away. Abandonment is one of the biggest problems in the church—people abandon what they once practiced and believed. They stop going to church, stop listening, stop learning, stop tithing, and start hardening their hearts. They stop evangelizing and start policing other people, arguing over their favorite pet peeve. Over time, they become lukewarm. They tend to be smart, capable, admirable people who got into pride because they were no longer connected to a church (they had a bad experience, got hurt, got offended), no longer accountable to a senior minister, and the devil sent them someone to speak what they wanted to hear.
    - I teach my children, "Ask yourself who is speaking." Not everybody is an expert on everything.
    - Just because an evangelist can get a million people to a crusade doesn't mean he's an expert on doctrine. An evangelist evangelizes. A pastor shepherds. A teacher teaches. Why would you expect an evangelist to be a good teacher just because he performs miracles?
    - Know what people are good at and learn from them. Ignore them when they depart from their lane.
    - I also tell my children, "Don't take financial advice from a broke person. Don't take health advice from a sick person. They will lead you the wrong way because that's all they know."
    - By honoring people's calling and gifts, we get the best out of people and avoid the worst out of them. If you have a habit of trusting the wrong people, you will be easily deceived in the end times.

8. **Lose fat and cut out refined sugar**. This should be the number 1 natural advice to Americans. America is the fattest country in the world. People who "eat right and exercise" struggle with their weight, energy, and well-being in America. Something is wrong.
    - I would start by cutting out all artificial sweeteners like high fructose corn syrup and "Zero" products.
    - I would fast at least 1 meal a day; I try to eat 2 meals a day unless I'm leading Bible tours. Three a day is too much for me. Eating so much makes me slow and eats up my time. **Proverbs 23:2** (NKJV) says, "And put a knife to your throat If you are a man given to appetite."
    - When I moved to Florida, I immediately found that I gained weight and built up those "love handles" even though I ate right and exercised. I prayed and asked the Lord about this. He showed me His design of the human body. Activating the vagus nerve would burn off my visceral fat—the fat that surrounds people's heart and organs and is difficult to get rid of. I interviewed a mega church pastor and one of the smartest functional medicine doctors about it. You can watch those interviews on my main channel:

    - Dr. Ben Bowers 1: REGENERATIVE HEALTH BREAKTHROUGHS - Highest IQ Doctor on Brain, Cancer, Diabetes, Fat Loss, Vagus;
    - Dr. Ben Bowers 2: 5 SUPER FOODS to Supercharge Your Microbiome & Heal Disease + COFFEE that Melts FAT; and on my backup channel

| Health Breakthroughs

- Dream Centre Pastor: ACTIVATE the VAGUS Nerve & BURN Visceral FAT | Lower Cortisol, Increase Energy & Youthfulness

Dream Centre Pastor

9. **Pay your tithes.** This is a sensitive topic that may evoke emotions. "That's just an Old Testament requirement," critics say. I can prove to you that it's not. It's an *end-time* issue, not a Mosaic Law issue. I don't see tithes the way some Christians do. The prophet Malachi predicted the coming of Elijah, the second coming of Jesus, and Judgment Day. These things are not in the past; they are futuristic. God is so gracious to give us a prelude ahead of time of what we will be held to account on the Day of Judgment. Two issues will be prominent on God's mind.

Malachi 3:2, 5-6, 8-12 (NKJV)

2 But who can endure the day of His coming? And who can stand when He appears?

5 And I will come near you for judgment; I will be a swift witness Against sorcerers, Against adulterers, Against perjurers...[after listing the most common sins, God zeroes in on two major end time issues.]

6 For I *am* the Lord, I do not change...[He made this statement to pre-empt the false accusation of men who claim "God has changed, He no longer cares about tithes and offerings."]

8 "Will a man rob God? Yet you have robbed Me! But you say, 'In what way have we robbed You?' In TITHES and OFFERINGS.

9 You are cursed with a curse, For you [believers at the Judgment Seat of Christ] have robbed Me, *Even* this whole nation.

10 Bring all the tithes into the storehouse, That there may be food in My house, And try Me now in this," Says the Lord of hosts,

"If I will not open for you the windows of heaven And pour out for you *such* blessing That *there will* not *be room* enough *to receive it.*

11 "And I will rebuke the devourer for your sakes, So that he will not destroy the fruit of your ground, Nor shall the vine fail to bear fruit for you in the field," Says the Lord of hosts;

12 "And all nations will call you blessed, For you will be a delightful land," Says the Lord of hosts.

People have many ways to justify their stinginess. God will not be mocked. He will hold each of us accountable for how we handled money—what we spent it on. 10% is an eternal tax to honor God; it blesses and protects the 90% we keep.

There is no protection over your business or finances without tithing. That's why a lot of Christians get into financial trouble. I've met them over the years; some of them have asked me for help. Before I can help anyone with money problems, the first question I ask them is, "Do you tithe faithfully?" In my experience, 95% don't.

Notice our tithe always goes to ministers of God's Word. There's no benefit giving the tithe to your children or to the poor—you're supposed to help them, that's good, but it doesn't count as tithe.

God says in verse 10, "Bring all the tithes into the storehouse, That there may be food in My house." Tithes always go to support full-time ministers working in the church or in ministry. If they're not preaching and teaching the Word, if they make light of the Bible and dismiss Bible prophecy, you'd be better off finding another minister to give to. Paul lays down the New Testament principle that you should tithe and offer to every minister who feeds you spiritually:

> **Galatians 6:6-7** (NET)
> Now the one who RECEIVES instruction in the word must SHARE all good things [referring to sowing money and resources] with the one who teaches it. **7** Do not be deceived. God will not be made a fool. For a person will reap what he sows [that's the

context of this famous verse on sowing—sow to teachers of the Word and stop supporting compromisers of the truth!]

10. **Serve your church.** Get involved in some active ministry. You were created for a purpose that connects you with the rest of the Body of Christ. You are needed and when you're "missing in action" (MIA), it creates stress and hard work for the rest of the Body.
    - This is the second issue God promised He will raise on Judgment Day. He knew ahead of time that the common temptation of end time believers would be getting distracted, tired, and making excuses.
    - "I'm burned out," I've heard church goers say. When I ask how much time they're serving, you can count less than 6 hours a week usually, and going to Church shouldn't count. Everyone is supposed to do that. You know what I found out? They're not burnt out from ministry; they're burnt out because they didn't make time for Bible reading and prayer. We're energized to serve by our relationship with God.

> **Malachi 3:13-15** (NKJV, these are words you will hear in the future at the Judgment Throne of God)
> "Your words have been harsh against Me," Says the LORD, "Yet you say, 'What have we spoken against You?' **14** You have said, 'It is useless to SERVE God; What profit is it that we have kept His ordinance, And that we have walked as mourners Before the LORD of hosts? **15** So now we call the proud blessed, For those who do wickedness are raised up; They even tempt God and go free.'"

These are words believers are saying against serving God. They may not say it to their pastor's face, but they say it within their hearts, "It's not worth it to serve God. The leaders don't notice me enough. I get more appreciation in the world. It's a waste of time to get to church early and prepare. Look how my friends who don't go to church drive a nicer car and live in a bigger home than me." When you compare yourself to someone in a moment of time, you can misjudge. You don't know the end of their life. I have seen those who serve God live better lives and end well. You don't know what's going to become of those who live for the devil. Just think of all the celebrities who didn't use their talents for God. How many of them lost everything? Despite having all the riches and fame the world could offer, they still ended up miserable.

That's not the life for me. It pays to obey God. Serving God is the highest honor in my life. The Lord takes notice of this when we have a good attitude towards church and ministry. Here's another end time prediction:

Malachi 3:16-18

Then those who feared the Lord spoke to one another, And the Lord listened and heard *them;* So a book of remembrance was written before Him For those who fear the Lord And who meditate on His name. **17** "They shall be Mine," says the Lord of hosts, "On the day that I make them My jewels. And I will spare them As a man spares his own son who serves him." **18** Then you shall again discern Between the righteous and the wicked, Between one who SERVES God And one who does NOT SERVE Him.

The Day of Judgment will make four classes of people clear:

a. The righteous—he who did *teshuvah,* i.e. repented and believed the Messiah;

b. The wicked—he who remained proud and relied on his own merits to save himself;
c. The one who serves God; and
d. The one who does not serve.

11. Go to a **Goshen**.
    ○ If you're the leader of a country, turn your country into a Goshen. Make sure it has food security, keep GMOs and the globalists out, and protect freedom of conscience, freedom of religion, and freedom of speech. On these foundations your country will flourish.
    ○ If you're a business leader or land owner, start turning your land into worship centers with places of refuge. Team up with good pastors who love prophecy and don't deny Jesus' Coming or the signs of the time.
12. Make **Jesus Christ your Lord and Savior** before Judgment Day comes. The Anti-Christ is temporary. The Tribulation is temporary. When this life is over, our permanent life begins. Our destiny cannot be changed once we breathe our last breath. The only permanent salvation comes from being set free from the curse of sin. People try to save themselves from their sins by keeping religious rules and laws, thus ignoring the grace of God. The Apostle Paul had an answer to this.

> **Galatians 2:21** (NKJV)
> I do not set aside the grace of God; for if righteousness [being right with God] comes through the law, then Christ died in vain.

If rule-keeping could wash away our sins, then Christ died in vain. He did not! The lie from the Garden of Eden to the

Tribulation is that we don't need God. We want to do things our own way. This planet proves doing things our own way is not going so well. We made lifeless idols into our gods. We looked to government as god. That's why we suffer in life. We don't know what we don't know. We don't do what we should do. To be set free, we need God to help us. God calls us to be humble, admit we're sinful, and accept the sacrifice of His Son Jesus on the Cross as the payment for our sins.

> **Proverbs 8:36** (NKJV)
> But he who sins against me wrongs his own soul;
> All those who hate me love death."

Choose life, not death. To be forgiven and accepted into the Family of God, pray this prayer out loud to God:

> *Dear Heavenly Father, I'm sorry for sinning against You. I cannot save myself. Thank You for sending Jesus to die and pay for my sins on the cross, I believe after 3 days, He rose again from the dead. He is alive! And He's living in me now. My life is not my own. I belong to You. Please prepare me to be a worthy child of God. Use my life to bring glory and honor to You. Thank you in Jesus' Name. Amen.*

Christopher Flanagan: Thank you for leading me to Christ, who freed me from addiction and saved my soul.

Email to tell us what God's done for you: info@discover.org.au. Welcome to the Family of God!

BESTSELLERS BY STEVE CIOCCOLANTI

30 Days to a New You
(Compact Plan for Personal Growth & Freedom)

A Guide to Making a Will
(Considering a church in your legacy)

From Buddha to Jesus
(Available in English, Chinese, French, Indonesian, Japanese, Spanish & Thai)

Get Prayers Answered
(#1 Prayer Book in America—30 years of answered prayers)

President Trump's Pro-Christian Accomplishments
(A faith-boosting record of the under-reported miracles God did in the White House)

The Divine Code: A Prophetic Encyclopedia of Numbers, Vol 1 & 2

(Discovering God Through Numbers from 1 to 1000)

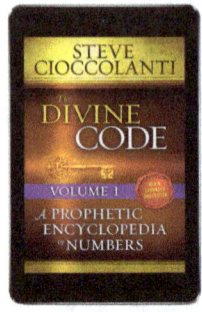
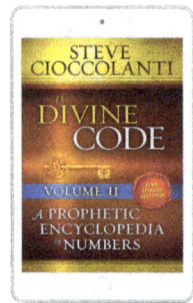

Scam Proof Your Life in the End Times

(Justice & Restoration for Christians)

TRUMP'S UNFINISHED BUSINESS:

10 PROPHECIES TO SAVE AMERICA

3 Editions: Hardcover, Softcover, Ebook

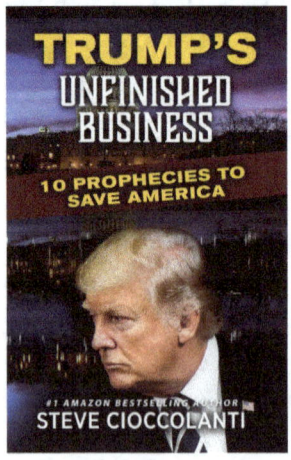

Ebooks are available through Amazon.com.

Bulk orders (25+) of *The 4 Horsemen of the Apocalypse* available upon request to info@discover.org.au

ACKNOWLEDGMENTS

A Christian company originally contacted me for this book to be written, then backed out as it was getting finished. The Lord told me it was part of His plan because He could spread His Word without needing central marketing or a central distributor. I am not against marketers or distributers—I work with both, but for this book, I am obliged to thank YOU, my dear reader, for believing in it and sharing it with friends. This book will reach countless hearts because of your grassroots efforts. Your action matters. Bulk orders (25+) are available upon request by emailing: info@discover.org.au.

The Discover Church family should also receive thanks for making this book a beautiful reality. The Lord has put a special group of Christians together and surrounded me with strong support which every author needs. Both my physical church and online church members contributed to the quality of this book and speed at which it was done to coincide with our 25th church anniversary.

My personal thanks to the members who stood by me during 15 days of round-the-clock writing and editing transcripts and notes that have been compiled over the course of 13 years: Alexis Cioccolanti, Andrew Nguon, Andrew Tam, Annie Lee Keller, Caren Chung, Julja Purcell, Kathleen Edwards, Kim Altemeyer, Lily Leong, Marla Nistico, Rod Bilderback, Selena Sok, Ser Pin Sim, and Terri Pierman.

| Believe & Belong: DiscoverChurch.Online

Online church does not mean a replacement of physical church. Conversely, physical church cannot do what online church can do. I believe in both. God wants both to reach the most. Thank you for choosing to activate your talents for Jesus in the last days.

Gift to readers who made it to the end!

Claim your Preppers eBook, **"The Safest Places During Global Famine or WW3"** at: www.DiscoverChurch.Online/Safe.

MEET STEVE CIOCCOLANTI

Steve Cioccolanti, B.A., M.Ed., is a seven-time #1 best-selling author on Amazon, a pioneer of online church, and a social media influencer. With over 70 million views, he is one of the most watched Christian YouTubers worldwide.

He founded Discover Church in Australia and celebrated 25 years of ministry at the time of this book's publication. In the next 10 years, his vision is to preach in all 50 states, and partner with pastors and business leaders to build Goshens (Christian communities with churches) worldwide.

Watch and subscribe here: www.YouTube.com/DiscoverMinistries

Having traveled to 60 nations, Pastor Cioccolanti leads life-changing, Christian tours to Israel, Jordan, Saudi Arabia, Thailand, Turkey, and beyond. He is a bold, prophetic voice on the topics of Israel, prophecy, justice, leadership, world religions and world missions.

He is currently authoring more books, filming more videos, and sharing prophetic wisdom to leaders around the world.

Join Partners Club
www.DiscoverChurch.Online/partner

Grow in Online Church
www.DiscoverChurch.online

Shop for Audios, Videos & Merch
www.DiscoverChurch.Online/shop

Contribute to World Missions
www.Discover.org.au/Give

Book Pastor Steve Cioccolanti for your church or event
contact: info@discover.org.au

Connect with Steve Cioccolanti on social media:

- patreon.com/cioccolanti
- amazon.com/author/newyorktimesbestseller
- youtube.com/DiscoverMinistries
- instagram.com/SteveCioccolanti
- facebook.com/discoverministry
- tiktok.com/@prayesutv
- x.com/cioccolanti

www.ingramcontent.com/pod-product-compliance
Lightning Source LLC
Chambersburg PA
CBHW070940230426
43666CB00011B/2509